BLOODY JUNGLE

0 11557 01208 8

BLOODY JUNGLE

The War in Vietnam

CHRIS EVANS

Foreword by Jim Ross

STACKPOLE
BOOKS

Copyright © 2013 by Chris Evans

Published by
STACKPOLE BOOKS
5067 Ritter Road
Mechanicsburg, PA 17055
www.stackpolebooks.com

Cover design by Caroline M. Stover

Printed in the United States of America

10 9 8 7 6 5 4 3 2 1

Library of Congress Cataloging-in-Publication Data

Evans, Chris (Chris R.)
  Bloody jungle : the war in Vietnam / Chris Evans ; foreword by Jim Ross.
      pages cm. — (Stackpole military photo series)
    ISBN 978-0-8117-1208-8
  1. Vietnam War, 1961–1975—Pictorial works. 2. Vietnam War, 1961–1975—
United States—Pictorial works. 3. United States—Armed Forces—History—
Vietnam War, 1961–1975—Pictorial works. I. Title.
  DS557.72.E93 2013
  959.704'30222—dc23
                                                                    2013030704

CONTENTS

FOREWORD

While the Vietnam War cut deeply into the soul of the nation and remains a lingering wound, the majority of those who participated upheld the mantra of honor-duty-country handed down and entrusted to them by their forefathers. They came from all walks of life and ethnic backgrounds. Many knew little or nothing of the backstory of the conflict; the threat of spreading communism seemed reason enough to pony up. But as the war escalated—employing misguided strategies and political manipulation—the challenges facing those slogging through the monsoon muck soon stood as insurmountable obstacles to a positive outcome. Worsening their plight, they became stereotyped as heartless killers on the home front and got little help from a South Vietnamese military content to let Americans do the heavy lifting—and dying. Over time, then, honor-duty-country boiled down to survive-and-go-home.

In spite of the confidence cultivated in training, few were prepared for the real horrors of war. Kill or be killed was only the first layer. Morality degraded quickly from exposure to unrelenting brutality and the push to stack enemy bodies like poker chips to be cashed in for victory. Soldiers saw buddies killed and maimed, and lived thereafter with the memory of their screams. They endured swarming insects, jungle rot, sleep deprivation, insufferable heat, friendly-fire incidents, and insidious booby-traps of every kind. They contended with a less-than-seasoned officer corps that rotated out of the field at twice the rate of enlisted men, as well as higher-ups who too often concocted "missions impossible" such as the infamous battles at Hamburger Hill and Firebase Ripcord.

Yet through it all, the bulk of the draftees and volunteers who served in Vietnam maintained a sense of personal honor, retained their love of country, and held the notion that somewhere in the morass some good would come from it all. And so they continued to march until the last combat units were withdrawn in 1973.

In spite of the fallout from such a life-changing event, most Vietnam veterans now live ordinary lives. They understand that the bell cannot be un-rung and have reconciled their combat experiences with what they know to be true. Though still taunted by demons from time to time, they manage to keep those subtle but hot embers at arm's length.

Included in this book are images from some of the survivors. They have opened their scrapbooks to share glimpses of their tours. Few things are of greater value to war veterans than these fading links to the most significant moments of their lives. As such, they reveal the camaraderie, the bravado, the hidden despair, and some of what they witnessed while prowling the lethal landscape there. Above all, they portray average young Americans trying to do their best while being forced to grow up too fast.

Jim Ross
Author of *Outside the Wire*

INTRODUCTION

The Vietnam War stands out in American history for its length, spanning nearly twenty years from the departure of the French shortly after their defeat at Dien Bien Phu on May 7, 1954; for its bloody cost—more than 58,000 American servicemen and women killed and more than 300,000 wounded; the cultural upheaval it spawned back home, including the killing of four university students at Kent State in Ohio by the Ohio National Guard; and the shocking culmination of hostilities on April 30, 1975, with the fall of Saigon to Communist forces.

This book aims to illustrate the war as seen through the camera lenses of the soldiers, airmen, Marines, and sailors who fought it. With the advent of inexpensive and readily available cameras and film, including instant processing using Polaroids, the Vietnam War was documented on a scale and with an intimacy never before seen by the public. Modern technology made the war bloody, its death toll augmented by the ever increasing sophistication of the weaponry employed, but it also sparked revolutionary care of the wounded. More salient, perhaps, is that the war bonded a generation of warriors together. And in that bond of shared sacrifice, of joys and sorrows, they captured their time together in Vietnam prolifically and often poignantly through photographs.

The photographs in *Bloody Jungle* are primarily from the warriors themselves. You'll see color Polaroids taken in the field on a dusty fire base and slides snapped from the cockpit of a Huey flying high over the jungle canopy. Some of the shots are blurred, others taken from odd angles and in poor lighting, and that is as it should be. If the book's raw approach unsettles, if the words of the combatants jar against the ear, then this book has served its small but important role in conveying a fraction of what it meant to fight in the Vietnam War.

Chris Evans
New York, New York
August 2013

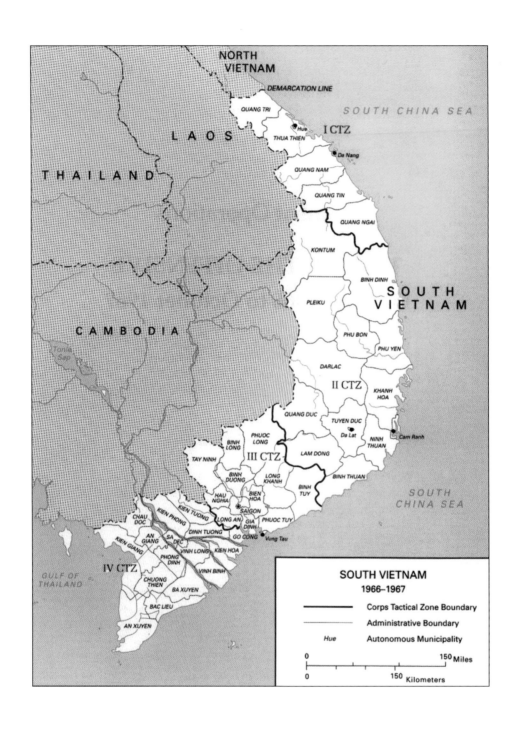

NORTH
VIETNAM

DEMARCATION LINE

QUANG TRI

SOUTH CHINA SEA

Hue

THUA THIEN

I CTZ

LAOS

Da Nang

QUANG NAM

THAILAND

QUANG TIN

QUANG NGAI

KONTUM

BINH DINH

SOUTH
VIETNAM

PLEIKU

PHU BON

PHU YEN

CAMBODIA

DARLAC

Tonle
Sap

II CTZ

KHANH
HOA

QUANG DUC

TUYEN DUC

Da Lat

NINH
THUAN

Cam Ranh

BINH
LONG

PHUOC
LONG

III CTZ

LAM DONG

TAY NINH

BINH
DUONG

LONG
KHANH

BINH
TUY

BINH THUAN

HAU
NGHIA

BIEN
HOA

SOUTH
CHINA SEA

CHAU
DOC

KIEN TUONG

KIEN PHONG

LONG AN

SAIGON

GIA
DINH

PHUOC TUY

AN
GIANG

SA
DEC

DINH TUONG

GO CONG

Vung Tau

KIEN GIANG

PHONG
DINH

VINH LONG

KIEN HOA

IV CTZ

CHUONG
THIEN

VINH BINH

GULF OF
THAILAND

BA XUYEN

BAC LIEU

AN XUYEN

SOUTH VIETNAM

1966–1967

━━━━━ Corps Tactical Zone Boundary

─────── Administrative Boundary

Hue Autonomous Municipality

0   150 Miles

0   150 Kilometers

CHAPTER 1
SOLDIERS AND MARINES

Sergeant Fish relaxes with a beer on the wall of a fortified watchtower. He holds his M16, the ubiquitous American weapon of the Vietnam War. The M16 fired a 5.56mm round, which was significantly lighter than the 7.62mm round fired by the rifle it replaced, the larger M14. August 1969.

A Marine returns from patrol in the bush. Troops often ditched their helmets for "boonie hats," which were significantly lighter and didn't obscure their hearing while patrolling in the jungle. The downside was the complete lack of armor protection for the head, but it was a trade-off many were happy to make. June 1970.

Command Sergeant Major Ted G. Arthurs, 173rd Airborne Brigade, May 1967 to May 1968

The Sky Soldiers of the 173rd Airborne were in the thick of the fighting in Vietnam while Ted Arthurs was there, humping eighty-pound rucksacks through triple-canopy jungle and chasing down the Viet Cong and North Vietnamese in the Central Highlands. As a sergeant major for a battalion of 800 men, it was Arthurs's job to see them through this jungle hell and get them back home again.

Ted Arthurs observes enemy POW being interrogated.

A concerned Ted Arthurs contemplates the heavy casualties suffered by his unit.

A "three-man" snake, which Arthurs's troops roasted and ate with gusto.

A soldier cradles his M14 rifle as he watches supplies being dropped from a C-130 Hercules transport during Operation Junction City, February 1967. The operation proved to be the largest airborne operation of the Vietnam War.

A sandbag-fortified watchtower provides American troops with an ideal vantage to overlook river traffic and the low-lying countryside. Such a tower would often be equipped with an M60 machine gun, binoculars, possibly a night scope, and field radio and manned by at least two soldiers. August 1969.

Three members of the 173rd Airborne Brigade are all smiles as they flash the peace sign for the camera. Despite the smiles, the 173rd suffered heavy casualties during the war, especially during the Battle of Dak To in November 1967 in the Central Highlands of South Vietnam.

Two more members of the 173rd Airborne Brigade pose with their MUTT (Military Utitlity Tactical Truck), which was often referred to by its predecessor's name of Jeep. An M60 machine gun is mounted on a single pedestal in the rear of the MUTT along with a radio. The arm brassard on the soldier in the background is that of an military policeman (MP).

Major Robert W. Black, U.S. Army Ranger, District Senior Military Advisor, Rach Kien Province, November 1967 to November 1968

I was the Advisor to the District Chief of Rach Kein District, Long An Province, Major Dong. He did not speak English. He took a primarily administrative roll in running his county-size area of what was 30,000 to 50,000-plus souls. Major Dong would defer to me, but I would also defer to him. The man had been fighting for twenty years and knew what he was about. Sadly, Major Dong would eventually be killed while on operations.

The Military Chief was Captain Ngi. He was a good man, strong leader, and brave, and he spoke excellent English. A former District Chief, he displeased a politician and lost his previous job. He was my primary Vietnamese companion. We did many operations together.

The soldiers I worked with were Regional Force Companies. They were meant to be the Home Guard of their communities. I believed that guarding the home meant going forth in search of enemy activity in the district and prevailed upon them to do so, providing them with critical material.

I had the 555 Regional Force Company in the north of my district and in the District Capital of Rach Kien. The 627 Regional Force Company was in a mud fort in the south. The 555 did not have an officer worth a damn. The 627 had a captain who was a strong

Major Robert Black arrives in Rach Kien, Vietnam, November 1967. Black, a decorated Army Ranger (Bronze Star, Silver Star), fought in the Korean War and would now apply his skills to helping the Army of the Republic of Vietnam fight against the Viet Cong.

Major Black decorates the *Bac-Si* (doctor or medic) of the 555th R.F. Company for Rach Kien in 1968.

leader. The two companies numbered slightly over 100 men each.

I also had a Provisional Recon Platoon who dressed in tiger-striped fatigues. These were hard-nosed troops, some former Viet Cong, good for scouting.

Finally, there was the National Police—White Shirts, called "White Mice." They went on some operations for interrogation of prisoners.

Abject poverty was the lot of these men. When I first came into the district, all of us were armed with non-automatic M1 carbines from World War II. The enemy had AK-47s. After we found a VC weapons cache, we traded those in the Saigon supply dumps for M16s. We brought in concrete and poured pads; then, using boards from 105mm ammo boxes, we built crude one-room huts that we used sheet-metal roofs on. This

was housing for as many of our troops as possible. We also put a catchment system in the marketplace and fifty-gallon drums in the troop area to provide drinking water after the monsoon rains.

My Ranger training and my battle experience during the Korean War were a great help to me. We did a number of night operations, ambushes, and raid ops. We could handle most VC units if we could catch them, but their road blocks and hit-and-run mortar attacks were often done so fast we never touched them. I had forty-nine mortar attacks on my small (one-street) town.

Poverty and lack of support touched every aspect of these men. The Vietnamese supply system was poor; supplies were frequently low. We were low priority for artillery or air support. I never had an Arty FO

Relations between American advisors and their South Vietnamese counterparts were often collegial and ones of mutual respect. Here Major Black shakes hands with Captain Ngi after a successful patrol.

(forward observer) or FAC (forward air controller) in battle with me. Some of my men were cowards; some were brave. They were like all others.

The Viet Cong and the NVA were highly disciplined and totally ruthless. They terrorized the civilian population into submission and support. They killed every South Vietnamese leader or potential leader they could find. There were two governments in my district, the South Vietnamese one and a shadow VC one. Through infiltration and intimidation, the

enemy had an effective intelligence system. It was so good that the U.S. Army would not share its plans with the South Vietnamese at the tactical level. The ARVN was like a separate force. Everything military that went on in that district (county) was to be coordinated with me, but it did not happen. Everyone roamed where and when they wanted. American units sometimes had firefights with each other. I was shot at one night by an ARVN Ranger battalion that was roaming through my district without my knowledge. It

Black and other American advisors return from a successful patrol. Relying on the skill and courage of foreign troops meant advisors had to bond with the troops they led and instill loyalty through smart tactical decisions and genuine concern for the men they commanded.

Being a military advisor was much more than simply teaching the South Vietnamese how to fight. Here Major Black cuts the ribbon to a new school.

Black's Airborne Ranger tab is distinctive with its red outline on black patch. During his career, Black would be awarded the Silver Star and three Bronze Stars, two of them for valor.

was like having warlords and their bands in residence. There were no fire zones and boundaries—that hindered pursuit.

When I went to South Vietnam, we had a proud army there. Then, as men completed tours and went home, they were replaced by those influenced by antiwar groups at home. Morale kept going down. It was a strange war. We could go out on an operation and fight a battle, then return exhausted to listen to news broadcasts about the antiwar demonstrations back home. It was clear the U.S. was not going to go into North Vietnam and win the war because of concerns about China. One could only wonder why that was not resolved before committing troops. I was there during Tet, and we kicked their butts. We never lost a battle but lost the war.

Reporter Walter Cronkite interviews the commanding officer of the 1st Battalion, 1st Marines, during the Battle of Hue City on February 20, 1968, during the height of the Tet Offensive. Based on his observations in Vietnam, Cronkite would read his now famous editorial on the air one week later suggesting America could not win the war.

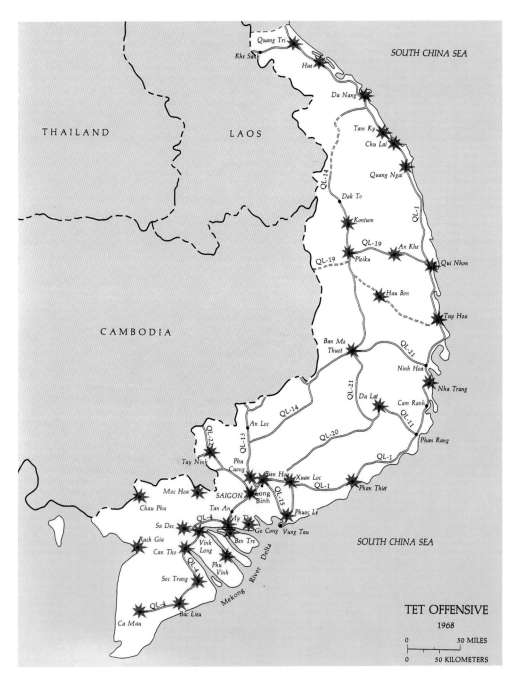

A Marine throws up a peace sign for the camera. Both men wear ERDL camouflage trousers, which consisted of four interlocking colors. This camouflage became standard for Marines in 1968, though a mix of clothing with olive-drab items continued to be used. November 1969.

A squad of Marines poses for the camera in a forward operating base. Each man wears a flak jacket, a ten-pound vest made up of layers of ballistic nylon and fiberglass plates. Unable to stop an AK-47 round (7.62mm) at close range, they were effective in protecting the torso and vital organs from shell fragments, snake bites, and bullets fired from longer distances.

Medal of Honor recipient Army Spec-4 Leslie H. Sabo Jr. during his tour in Vietnam with Company B, 3rd Battalion, 506th Infantry, 101st Airborne Division. On May 10, 1970, Sabo and his platoon were ambushed in eastern Cambodia by a large enemy force. Time and again, Sabo attacked the enemy and shielded his fellow soldiers from grenade blasts. Ignoring multiple gunshot and shrapnel wounds, Sabo charged and destroyed an enemy bunker, losing his life in the process. Because the reports of his heroism were lost, he wasn't awarded the Medal of Honor until May 16, 2012.

U.S. ARMY / GEORGE SABO

Members of the 3rd Battalion, 12th Infantry Regiment, 4th Infantry Division, "take five" during bunker construction on Hill 530, November 25, 1967. The 4th Infantry Division fought in the Central Highlands of South Vietnam along the border with Cambodia. In 1970 it crossed the border in what became known as the Cambodian Incursion.

A Marine by a rough and ready bunker of sandbags and plastic sheeting in a forward operating base. The design of the bunker suggests rapid construction. If the Marines were to stay there for longer than a few days, it's likely the bunker would be expanded and reinforced. June 1970.

Explosions mark the destruction of a Viet Cong tunnel and bunker site found by Marines during Operation Georgia, a coordinated assault with ARVN and South Vietnamese Popular Forces in the An Hoa area. The final tally for Operation Georgia was 103 VC killed against 9 Marines lost. May 5, 1966. USMC

In this series of shots, Marines take turns posing with an unexploded 122mm rocket that landed in their base, December 1968. Their smiles no doubt express their relief that the rocket, with forty pounds of high explosives inside, did not go off.

Staff Sergeant David P. Walker, LRP (Long-Range Patrol)

We'd just resumed our movement forward when what seemed to be the whole world erupted in gunfire and explosions. An increasingly intense volume of the funny little green things was coming our way, as well as what Sergeant Caughorn loudly identified as 82mm mortar impacts. I was in a half-crouch, attempting to better scan my area and having a genuine ball firing up my area of responsibility, when, from out of nowhere, what felt like a Louisville Slugger whacked the left side of my face.

Team 2-1, F/58 LRP, Bien Hoa, December 1967. Standing, left to right: Caughorn, Dave Walker, Fleck, Sachs. Kneeling: Wilson.

Heavy N/75 team awaiting infil bird. Arrow points to Walker.

I lost consciousness for what must have been a matter of only mere seconds, reawakening to green tracers flying over me. Still on my back, I groggily retrieved my weapon and blindly returned fire where I hoped the green things were originating. The ejected hot brass from my weapon struck my neck and dropped into my open fatigue shirt collar.

When things went relatively silent again, Jim Fleck, Sergeant Caughorn, and Ranger Brown were on me within seconds, and despite their jokes, it was obvious in their eyes that things weren't so hot. Ranger Brown immediately contacted Long Binh for a medevac chopper.

N/75 Ranger gate sign.

Team Hotel infilled in Nui Mieus, April 1971.

We touched down at the 24th Evacuation Hospital in Long Binh, where two medics and a Catholic chaplain awaited me with a gurney. In a well-meaning gesture, the chaplain inquired as to whether I desired last rites. Well, this hadn't been one of my better days, and I spitefully told the chaplain that, first off, I was a Protestant, and second, I had no plans for growing angel wings or stoking hell's fires in the near future.

Larry Chambers (left) in 1969 with Gary Linderer, one of his closest friends. The two were on the same six-man long-range reconnaissance patrol (LRP) team with Company L, 75th Rangers, 101st Airborne Division in Vietnam from 1968 to 1969. Chambers was awarded a Purple Heart, two Bronze Stars (one for valor), two Air Medals with "V" device (combat with an enemy force), the Combat Infantryman's Badge, the Parachutist Badge, the Army Commendation Medal, and the Vietnam Cross of Gallantry. Linderer was awarded two Purple Hearts, two Silver Stars, the Bronze Star with V (for valor), and the Army Commendation Medal with "V." Both Chambers and Linderer went on to publish several successful books about their experiences in Vietnam. LARRY CHAMBERS

Christmas Day, 1968, near Loc Ninh. A crewmember of an M113 armored personnel carrier sits by his vehicle's .50-caliber machine gun.

Two soldiers man a sandbagged roadside outpost. They are well armed with a pair of M16 rifles and an M79 grenade launcher, in addition to a radio as well as what appears to be an AN/PVS 2 Starlight Night Scope.

Lieutenant Colonel Hal Moore, commander of the 1st Battalion, 7th Cavalry, on the radio during the fight for LZ X-Ray in the Ia Drang Valley of Vietnam. The second photo is that of a wounded soldier from Moore's unit. The Battle of the Ia Drang Valley took place between November 14 and 18, 1965, and was the first major clash between American forces and units of the North Vietnamese Army. These photos were extracted from U.S. Army motion-picture footage. U.S. ARMY

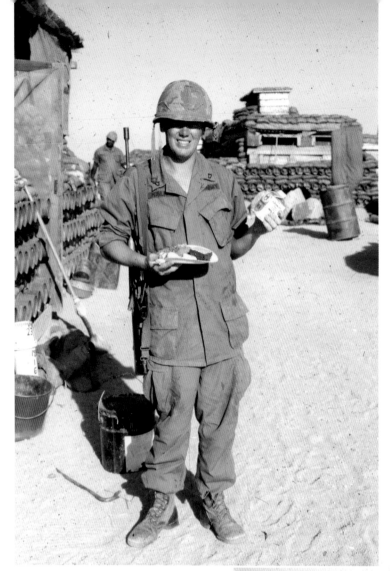

A soldier smiles at a fire base while holding his lunch. He has good reason to smile: he has cold milk and a hot meal—something not possible out in the bush. June 1969.

As the war progressed, the reasons for fighting it became murky for an increasing number of draftees who found themselves thousands of miles from home in a land they knew next to nothing about. The proliferation of peace signs like the one worn by the Marine on the right served as a subtle yet clear protest.

Sergeant David E. Weimer prepares to go into the field with Company A, Reconnaissance Battalion, April 10, 1967. Weimer served as a still photographer with the photo lab at Phu Bai, 3rd Marine Division. USMC

President Lyndon B. Johnson in Vietnam with the top soldier in theater, Gen. William Westmoreland, December 23, 1967. Westmoreland, a World War II combat veteran, rose quickly through the ranks and was considered to be one of the U.S. Army's best and brightest. His command in Vietnam was known for its positive assessments of the war even as public sentiment back home grew increasingly negative. U.S. ARMY

**Lieutenant Michael Lee Lanning,
Platoon Leader, Recon Platoon Leader,
and Rifle Company Commander in the
2nd Battalion, 3rd Infantry Regiment,
199th Light Infantry Brigade, in Vietnam
from April 1969 to April 1970**

Nearly twenty years after my return home from Vietnam, I began to write about the experience. My first book, *The Only War We Had: A Platoon Leader's Journal of Vietnam* (Reprint. College Station, TX: Texas A&M University Press, 2007), opened with an introduction about how I felt then and still do today, some four decades after my service in the war. I wrote:

A war is a major event in a man's life. It was popular among many who fought to say that Vietnam "wasn't much of a war, but it was the only one we had." I can only add that it was enough of a war for me, for I am neither old nor young enough to want to experience another one.

Drying our gear after a night ambush in the Delta region near Binh Chanh in June 1969.

I am proud to have served in Vietnam. I feel no guilt, have no regrets, harbor no memories I cannot cope with, and—except for a few terrifying moments and the many young men resting for eternity under neat rolls of military headstones—I would change nothing.

What I do feel is satisfaction and pride in doing what had to be done, in standing up when called upon by my country and in being prepared to die if necessary.

I may have been naïve in my love for and feeling of obligation to my country. My attitude was that the USA had been good to me; now it was time to pay a little back. The elected officials said the war was right and I had a duty to fight. That was enough for me.

However, I went to Vietnam not only because of the obligation I felt to do my duty but also because I did not want to miss the chance to experience the major significant

Preparing to assault an NVA base camp southwest of Xuan Loc in November 1969.

event of my generation. I, of course, wondered what it would be like to go to war, and I dreaded the prospects of hardship, discipline, family separation, and the possibility of death or debilitating injuries. Yet I knew I did not want to let pass the opportunity to challenge myself and to experience the adventure. I felt it would be an irreversible mistake to avoid the war, for I knew if I did, I would never know myself to the fullest.

Upon arrival in Vietnam, I quickly learned that it was nothing like the movies about war that I had watched on the big screen. Instead of grizzled old sergeants with greying hair and cigar stubs in their mouth, I found my platoon in Charlie Company, 2nd Battalion, 3rd Infantry, 199th Light Infantry Brigade, to be led, because of recent casualties, by two spec fours—who alternated being in charge. I also quickly learned the tremendous burden of responsibility for

Artillery Fire Support Base Crystal west of Xuan Loc in December 1970.

the welfare and lives of my men. Blood spilt by soldiers in one's command produces stains that do not wash away from one's body and mind despite the passage of time.

It did not take long to also discover that the grunt riflemen experienced far more hardships and dangers than their fellow soldiers in the rear. Infantrymen quickly learned to dislike the rear echelon troops almost as much as the draft dodgers back home. At times it seemed we had more disdain for those comfortably living in rear compounds as we did for our enemy who suffered the same as we.

Not all was bad. The comraderie between fellow warriors nurtured on the battlefield lasts far beyond the rice paddies and jungles and now into our old age. The thrill and satisfaction of walking the battlefield with fellow soldiers after a successful fight is something the protected will never know.

Less than two months after my twenty-third birthday, I assumed command of Bravo Company in the same battalion—detailed in my second book, *Vietnam*

1969–1970: A Company Commander's Journal. Within days I had the privilege of leading more than a hundred soldiers in combat—and being able to employ the vast supporting fires of the U.S. military. After maneuvering my platoons into advantageous positions to fix the enemy, my artillery forward observer began to control from one to four batteries of six guns each. After several volleys, multiple Cobra gunships rolled in with rockets and machine-gun fire. When their loads were extinguished, an Air Force observer flying overhead followed my orders to bring in a flight of two or more F-4 delivering napalm and bombs. While orchestrating all this fire power, the thought of taxpayer expense never crossed my mind. Spending thousands, often hundreds of thousands, of taxpayer dollars to protect my men and eliminate the enemy seemed more than responsible to me. The joys, accomplishments, and heartbreaks remain as vivid today as they were more than four decades ago. Yet I continue to have no apologies and no regrets. I am not wounded nor broken; therefore, I do not need to heal.

Members of Company C, 1st Battalion, 8th Infantry Regiment, 1st Brigade, 4th Infantry Division, descend the side of Hill 742, located five miles northwest of Dak To during Operation MacArthur, November 14 to 17, 1967. The Battle of Dak To ran from November 2 to 22, 1967, in the Central Highlands of South Vietnam and formed part of the "Border Battles" at that time.

A famous photograph of Sgt. Ronald A. Payne of Atlanta, Georgia, a squad leader in Company A, 1st Battalion, 5th Mechanized Infantry, 25th Infantry Division, checking a tunnel entrance before entering it to search for Viet Cong and their equipment during Operation Cedar Falls, January 24, 1967.

A team of engineers prepares to place a bundle of C4 explosives in a Viet Cong tunnel. During the war, the American military tried several different methods to destroy these tunnels, including blowing acetylene gas into them and then igniting the vapors. When the tunnels ran too deep for this method, explosives were used, often combined with sacks of C2 riot-control powder, which would saturate the tunnels and keep the Viet Cong from reusing them for months.

The MX991/U 90-degree-angle head flashlight was made of a waterproof plastic base and powered by two replaceable D-cell batteries. Colored filters for the lens were stored in a compartment below the batteries. The design for the flashlight debuted during World War II, although the original was made of painted brass.

A Marine patrol sweeps for land mines along a dirt road. Previous victims of Viet Cong sappers include a truck and an LVTP-V.

The same patrol. A Marine walks past the rusting remains of a truck that was destroyed by a land mine.

The importance of holding the high ground is evident in this photo. From his vantage point, the soldier has an uninterrupted view of the land around the hill where the forward operating base has been built. September 1968.

A Marine and a soldier pose casually in these two photos, their M16s in their hands. The prevalence of cameras in the field and the irregular pace of combat in Vietnam meant that young men could capture their time as warriors for posterity.

Air Force Office of Special Investigations (OSI) agent Senior Airman Richard D. Emmons (left) and Republic of Korea Army Colonel Lee (right) display weapons captured from the enemy near Phu Cat Air Base. Though not part of the Security Police, Air Force OSI agents gathered valuable intelligence that helped in the defense of U.S. Air Force air bases. U.S. AIR FORCE

Enemy RPG and rocket rounds as well as hand grenades, bullets, and mines. The RPG-7 (or B-50 for the North Vietnamese license-built variant) fired a rocket-propelled antitank grenade and is considered a short-range weapon, with relative accuracy dropping off after 100 meters. August 1972.

Various items captured from Viet Cong soldiers, including sun helmets, shirts, canteens, eating utensils, and weapons. November 1969.

A destroyed North Vietnamese PT-76 amphibious armored vehicle is inspected by U.S. troops at Ben Het Special Forces Camp after the only tank-versus-tank encounter between American and North Vietnamese forces during the war. On the night of March 3, 1969, elements of the 1st Battalion, 69th Armored Regiment, engaged a force of PT-76s of the 16th Company, 4th Battalion, 202nd Armored Regiment, of the North Vietnamese Army. In the ensuing battle, two American tank crew were killed while two North Vietnamese PT-76s and one armored personnel carrier were destroyed. Armor-on-armor clashes wouldn't happen again until South Vietnamese M-41 tanks fought NVA tanks in Laos in March 1971.

Suspected Viet Cong with bags over their heads and some with their arms tied are interrogated for information. Trying to determine enemy from friend was exceptionally difficult in Vietnam, especially with the Viet Cong, unlike the North Vietnam Army regulars, who wore uniforms.

The North Vietnamese pith helmet was a design based on an earlier French model. Made of naturally occurring pith and later cork, the helmet offered protection from the sun, but none from shrapnel and bullets.

A Chinese-made NVA AK-47 chest bandoleer. Worn across the chest, the pouch provided quick access to the magazines inside while providing a modicum of protection at the same time.

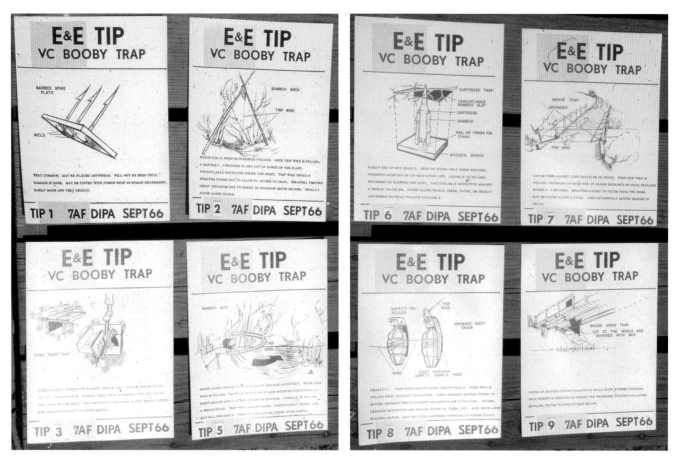

Instructional notices warning about the different types of booby traps employed by the Viet Cong. For most American troops in Vietnam, the jungle was a foreign and forbidding place full of natural dangers like snakes and spiders. The Viet Cong's use of ingeniously hidden booby traps that could kill or maim only added to their fear, loathing, and mistrust of the jungle.

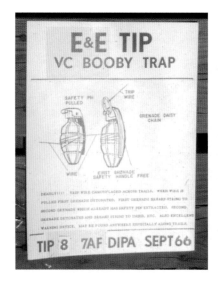

Just one example of the many booby traps that faced American forces during the Vietnam War. The Viet Cong were industrious in taking salvaged weapons and ammunition that American troops lost and using it against its former owners.

The body of a dead Viet Cong soldier is loaded onto a truck after a failed VC attack against an American base. The treatment of Viet Cong and North Vietnamese Army dead was far less solemn and respectful than that accorded to American and allied personnel dead. One contributing factor to this attitude was the American high command's focus on obtaining a "body count" as a means of quantifying victories in a war where land wasn't conquered and permanently held and large-scale, set-piece battles were rare.

Viet Cong prisoners are brought in for questioning after battle. It was American policy to hand over all prisoners to the South Vietnamese. This, however, lead to numerous challenges that would continue throughout the war. The handling and interrogation of prisoners, along with general interactions with the civilian population in a guerrilla war where friend and foe were difficult to distinguish, made it important for the American military to grapple with its legal policy in conjunction with the Geneva Convention and American and Vietnamese laws. It is worth noting that neither the United States nor North Vietnam declared a state of war, and North Vietnam refused to acknowledge the Viet Cong as part of their regime while the South Vietnam government considered them criminals. Further complicating matters, North Vietnam viewed captured American pilots as pirates and did not accord them prisoner of war status.

"THE ENEMY IN YOUR HANDS"
(Reproduction of 3x5 card of instructions issued to all troops.)

THE ENEMY IN YOUR HANDS

AS A MEMBER OF THE US MILITARY FORCES, YOU WILL COMPLY WITH THE GENEVA PRISONER OF WAR CONVENTIONS OF 1949 TO WHICH YOUR COUNTRY ADHERES. UNDER THESE CONVENTIONS:

YOU CAN AND WILL

DISARM YOUR PRISONER
IMMEDIATELY SEARCH HIM THOROUGHLY
REQUIRE HIM TO BE SILENT
SEGREGATE HIM FROM OTHER PRISONERS GUARD HIM CAREFULLY
TAKE HIM TO THE PLACE DESIGNATED BY YOUR COMMANDER

YOU CANNOT AND MUST NOT

MISTREAT YOUR PRISONER
HUMILIATE OR DEGRADE HIM
TAKE ANY OF HIS PERSONAL EFFECTS WHICH DO NOT HAVE SIGNIFICANT MILITARY VALUE
REFUSE HIM MEDICAL TREATMENT IF REQUIRED AND AVAILABLE

ALWAYS TREAT YOUR PRISONER HUMANELY

KEY PHRASES

ENGLISH	VIETNAMESE
Halt	Dung lai
Lay down your gun	Buong sung xuong
Put up your hands	Dua tay len
Keep your hands on your head	Dua tay len dau
I will search you	Tai kham ong
Do not talk	Dung noi chuyen
Walk there	Lai dang kia
Turn Right	Xay ben phai
Turn Left	Xay ben trai

"The courage and skill of our men in battle will be matched by their magnanimity when the battle ends. And all American military action in Vietnam will stop as soon as aggression by others is stopped"

21 August 1965   Lyndon B. Johnson

THE ENEMY IN YOUR HANDS

1. HANDLE HIM FIRMLY, PROMPTLY, BUT HUMANELY
The captive in your hands must be <u>disarmed, searched</u>, secured and watched. But he must also be treated at all times as a human being. He must not be tortured, killed, mutilated, or degraded, even if he refuses to talk. If the captive is a woman, treat her with all respect due her sex.

2. TAKE THE CAPTIVE QUICKLY TO SECURITY
As soon as possible evacuate the captive to a place of safety and interrogation designated by your commander. Military documents taken from the captive are also sent to the interrogators, but the captive will keep his personal equipment except weapons.

3. MISTREATMENT OF ANY CAPTIVE IS A CRIMINAL OFFENSE. EVERY SOLDIER IS PERSONALLY RESPONSIBLE FOR THE ENEMY IN HIS HANDS
It is both dishonorable and foolish to mistreat a captive. It is also a punishable offense. Not even a beaten enemy will surrender if he knows his captors will torture or kill him. He will resist and.make his capture more costly. Fair treatment of captives encourages the enemy to surrender.

4. TREAT THE SICK AND WOUNDED CAPTIVE AS BEST YOU CAN
The captive saved may be an intelligence source. In any case he is a human being and must be treated like one. The soldier who ignores the sick and wounded degrades his uniform.

5. ALL PERSONS IN YOUR HANDS, WHETHER SUSPECTS, CIVILIANS, OR COMBAT CAPTIVES, MUST BE PROTECTED AGAINST VIOLENCE, INSULTS, CURIOSITY, AND REPRISALS OF ANY KIND
Leave punishment to the courts and judges. The soldier shows his strength by his fairness, firmness, and humanity to the persons in his hands.

A Viet Cong soldier stands beneath a Viet Cong flag carrying his AK-47 rifle. He was participating in the exchange of POWs by the Four Power Joint Military Commission on February 12, 1973.

Despite little formal training in most cases, the Viet Cong proved a fierce and relentless foe. Here, in 1968, a simply clad VC crouches in a bunker while holding a 7.62mm semi-automatic SKS rifle. Designed by Russia during World War II, the SKS was exported widely and license-built in many Soviet bloc countries.

Two Viet Cong and a North Vietnamese Army officer with still and motion-picture cameras that they will use to photograph the exchange of prisoners of war, February 2, 1973.

Viet Cong soldiers carry a litter with injured American POW Capt. David Earle Baker (captured June 27, 1972) from the hospital tent to the release point. American and South Vietnamese prisoners were exchanged for Viet Cong and North Vietnamese prisoners on February 12, 1973. U.S. ARMY

CHAPTER 3
DUST OFF

This remarkable sequence of photographs details the immediate aftermath of a land mine exploding underneath an army two-and-a-half-ton truck in March 1966. The force of the explosion was great enough to buckle the heavy frame of the truck, indicating the mine was an antitank device.

The wounded are tended to beside the truck before being carried by stretcher to a Huey air ambulance, known by the code name Dust Off during the war. A Huey gunship flies cover overhead in the fourth photo while the Dust Off lands. In moments, the wounded are loaded aboard and whisked away to immediate emergency treatment, typically arriving within an hour of being wounded. This rapid evacuation saved countless lives, but also resulted in heavy casualties among the Dust Off crews, who regularly flew into firefights in order to get the wounded out.

The 93rd Evacuation Hospital at
Long Binh, South Vietnam, 1966. An
estimated 11,000 women served in
Vietnam during the conflict, with the
vast majority of them in the nursing
and medical field.

First Lieutenant Elaine H. Niggemann
changes a surgical dressing for James J.
Torgelson at the 24th Evacuation
Hospital, July 9, 1971.

With the advent of better protective gear such as the flak jacket and the ability to treat battlefield casualties quickly, many more soldiers survived what would have been fatal wounds in earlier conflicts. It was important, however, that soldiers wear their gear properly, as noted in a report by the U.S. Army Surgeon General after the war:

The rapid fire weapons of the enemy (Viet Cong and NVA) resulted in a significant increase over World War II and Korea in the percentages of multiple wounds among the distribution of wounds by site.

Small arms fire caused approximately two-thirds of the wounds of the head and neck, and three-fourths of the trunk wounds; fragments accounted for the remainder. Fragments and small arms contributed fairly equally to wounds of the extremities.

Twenty to thirty percent of the penetrating head wounds brought in from the field in Vietnam were classed as "expectant" cases, and little could have been done for them; however, the mortality rate for the others was rather low because of early evacuation, extensive use of blood, and the presence of fully trained neurosurgeons in the combat zone. Most of the abdominal fatalities were from extensive liver destruction or multiple organ involvement.

To quote Lieutenant Colonel (later Colonel) William M. Hammon, MC: "If our combat troops . . . were to wear the helmet, we believe that about ⅓ fewer significant combat casualties would need to be admitted to a neurosurgical center here in Vietnam." Flak vests did prove effective against three-fourths of the fragments which struck the thorax, thereby increasing the percentage of gunshot wounds to other areas of the body to 75 percent of chest wounds.

Troops, in static positions or in air or ground vehicles, usually wore both helmets and flak vests, but soldiers on the move found the body armor too heavy and too hot. Some commanders (and some individuals regardless of the command decision) decided to forego the protection rather than accept the reduction in mission capability and the increase in heat casualties.

PERCENT OF DEATHS AND WOUNDS BY AGENT, U.S. ARMY, IN WORLD WAR II, KOREA, AND VIETNAM

Agent	Deaths			Wounds		
	World War II	Korea	Vietnam*	World War II	Korea	Vietnam*
Small arms	32	33	51	20	27	16
Fragments	53	59	36	62	61	65
Booby traps, mines	3	4	11	4	4	15
Punji stakes	—	—	—	—	—	2
Other	12	4	2	14	8	2

*January 1965 to June 1970.
Source: Statistical Data on Army Troops Wounded in Vietnam, January 1965–June 1970, Medical Statistics Agency, Office of the Surgeon General, U.S. Army.

The two combatants. The Russian AK-47 used by the Viet Cong and North Vietnamese Army was a rugged and easy-to-use assault rifle that fired a 7.62mm bullet capable of hitting its target out to over 400 yards. The American Colt M16 assault rifle fired a significantly smaller 5.56mm round with a longer accurate range out to 600 yards. The M16 suffered from jamming issues early on, especially as the weapon was initially believed to not need cleaning. With proper care and improved design, the M16 grew ever more reliable, and like the AK-47, variants remain in production to this day.

Captain Michael Harvey, U.S. Army MP, inspects an AK-47 in Vietnam, 1968. It's worth noting that the magazine has been incorrectly inserted. U.S. ARMY HERITAGE AND EDUCATION CENTER

Members of the 2nd Squad, 4th Platoon, Company D, 3/8, 1st Brigade, move forward returning fire in a firefight during Operation MacArthur in the Central Highlands, November 1967.

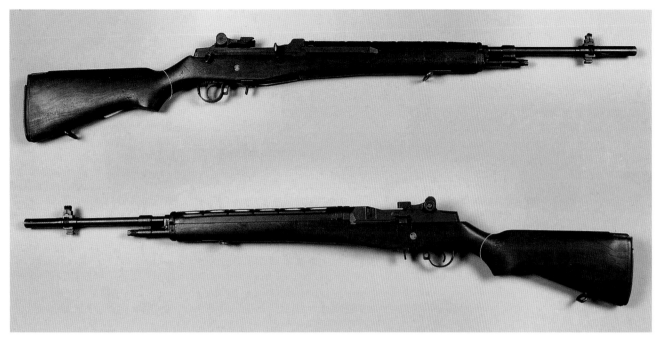

The M14 rifle was replaced by the M16 as the standard weapon of the soldier and Marine during the course of the Vietnam War. Though the power of its larger 7.62mm round meant it could hit harder and blast through cover in the jungle with greater ease, the M14 was heavy at nine pounds and awkward in the confined space of the jungle because of its length.

The M1911 semi-automatic pistol was the standard sidearm for American forces in Vietnam. Firing a .45 ACP bullet, the M1911 had respectable stopping power, but was typically used only in extreme situations when the enemy was very close.

The M7 bayonet mated to the M16 provided the soldier with both a spear-like stabbing weapon and a fighting knife when not attached to his rifle.

The AN PVS-2 Starlight Night Vision Scope was a first-generation night-sighting device operated by taking in ambient light and amplifying it by up to 1,000 times to turn "night into day" for the shooter looking through the scope. To function at full capacity, the scope needed moonlight. Later-generation night scopes would use infrared.

Specialist-4 Richard Champion, squad leader, Company B, 4th Battalion, 21st Infantry, 11th Light Infantry Brigade, shouts instructions to his squad after receiving sniper fire while on patrol on Hill 56, seventy miles southeast of Chu Lai, January 19, 1971.

The M69 flak jacket was a vest made of several layers of ballistic nylon that acted to stop shrapnel and slower-moving projectiles. These vests were not designed to stop—nor could they—a 7.62mm round fired by an AK-47. Earlier models used manganese steel plate, but this made the vest extremely heavy.

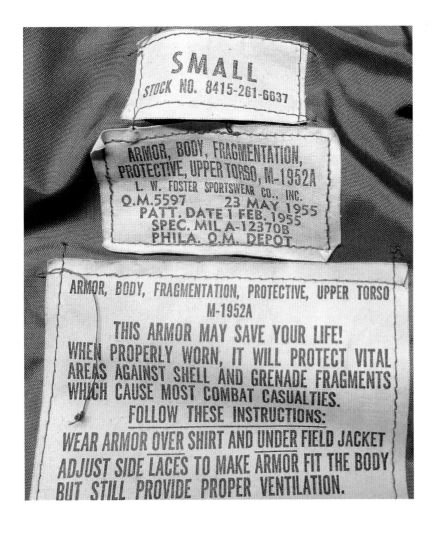

Flak jackets came with warning labels instructing the soldier and Marine how to wear it properly. This example is from a Marine M1955 model, but the warnings were similar in all models.

U.S. Air Force Security Police in combat at Tan Son Nhut during the Tet Offensive in 1968. Enemy troops had breached the perimeter and made it onto the runway. After intense fighting that lasted through the night, the Security Police and U.S. and South Vietnamese Army troops repelled the enemy. U.S. AIR FORCE

Operation Oregon, a search-and-destroy mission conducted by an infantry platoon of Troop B, 1st Reconnaissance Squadron, 9th Cavalry, 1st Cavalry Division (Airmobile), three kilometers west of Duc Pho, Quang Ngai Province, April 24, 1967. An infantryman is lowered into a tunnel by members of the reconnaissance platoon. U.S. ARMY

An M60 machine gun mounted facing rearward on an M113 of Bravo Troop, 3rd Squadron, 4th Cavalry, November 1968. Note the box of C rations inside the carrier. The M60, often called the "Pig" because of its weight of 23 pounds, fired the heavier 7.62mm bullet and could provide cover fire out to 1,200 yards.

M60 gunner Scott Bing, festooned with belts of 7.62mm ammunition, stands at ease with his weapon. The life of a gunner was dangerous as the enemy would focus their fire on the rapid-firing machine gun in hopes of knocking it out.

A1C David Shark with his sentry dog
Heino at Cam Ranh Bay Air Base,
South Vietnam. It is not possible to
overestimate the incredible bond that
existed between handler and dog. The
handler trusted the dog with his life,
and the dog was absolutely loyal, even
to the death. U.S. AIR FORCE

Lance Corporal Ralph H. McWilliams and
his scout dog, Major, November 1967.

Members of the 2nd Squad,
4th Platoon, Company D, 3/8,
1st Brigade, move forward,
returning fire during a
firefight during Operation
MacArthur in the Central
Highlands, November 1967.

Clad only in shorts and sandals, a soldier mans an M60 machine gun on top of a sandbagged bunker. The extreme temperatures in Vietnam and the sporadic nature of the fighting led troops to seek comfort over safety during the lulls between combat. June 1969.

The U.S. Army M1966 jungle boot featured several improvements over earlier all-leather models for the tropical conditions of Vietnam. With cotton canvas duck uppers (later nylon), small air inlets, and a Vibram rubber sole, the boot performed very well. It was eventually improved further with a stainless steel plate in the sole of the boot to prevent injuries from punji sticks.

Looking like an igloo made out of green snow, this sandbag bunker sports an M60 machine gun in its position defending the perimeter of a firebase. August 1969.

A fortified guard tower overlooks a rice paddy. These sandbags are of the earlier cloth type and were easily stacked. Later versions were plastic and had a tendency to slip and not stay in place, making it more difficult to stack them.

The Russian-built RPK (Ruchnoy Pulemyot Kalashnikova) was similar in its inner workings to the AK-47 and also fired the 7.62mm round.

An M2 .50-caliber machine gun on a tripod on the roof of a bunker. With an effective range of 1,800 yards, the M2 packed a potent punch. Weighing over 80 pounds meant it was typically used in static defense or mounted on vehicles.

A soldier of the 1st Infantry Division, known as the Big Red One, wades through a muddy river while holding an M79 40mm grenade launcher. The M79 was affectionately called "Thumper" and "Blooper" by the troops because of the sound made when the grenade fired. The launcher could accurately hit a target out to around 400 yards. Slow to reload, the M79 was eventually replaced by attaching the grenade tube under the barrel of the M16.

The M79 weighed just under six pounds empty. Unlike the magazine-fed M14 and M16, the M79 was a single-shot, break-action weapon that loaded from the breach.

The importance of teaching draftees how to keep their weapons clean and functioning in a jungle environment spurred the U.S. military to create simple, easy to read instruction manuals drawn like comic books.

The M72 LAW (light antitank weapon) was a 66mm rocket launcher and the standard soldier-carried antitank weapon of the U.S. Marines and U.S. Army. The warhead was capable of penetrating eight inches of steel.

The M61 fragmentation grenade weighed 13.75 ounces and was designed to maim and kill personnel. Anyone standing within sixteen feet of an explosion could well be killed.

The M18 colored smoke grenade was used for signaling throughout the Vietnam War.

A well-equipped bunker expecting action. From left to right are 40mm grenades for an M79 Blooper, two boxes of belts of 7.62mm ammunition for an M60 machine gun, and flares.

The M18A1 Claymore was an antipersonnel mine that was positioned above the ground and fired by remote control by means of a wire connected to a firing switch.

Inside the mine were approximately 700 steel pellets that would fly out like a shotgun burst when the C4 explosive in the mine was detonated.

The AN/PRC 77 radio entered service in Vietnam in 1968, replacing the AN/PRC 25. One of the main differences was the elimination of vacuum tubes for solid-state components. It had a range of approximately five miles, but this varied tremendously depending on location and conditions.

An M29 81mm mortar crew relax in their weapon pit between fire missions. Cans of beer and a reel-to-reel tape deck on the sandbags suggest they aren't expecting enemy fire. The M29 was an improved version of the World War II M1 81mm mortar. Able to fire high-explosive shells out to 5,000 yards, the M29 could also fire white-phosphorous shells and illumination rounds that when fired would give off 500,000 candle power of white light while suspended from a small parachute. These rounds could take over a minute to fall back to earth, giving American forces bright light to see attacking Viet Cong and NVA at night.

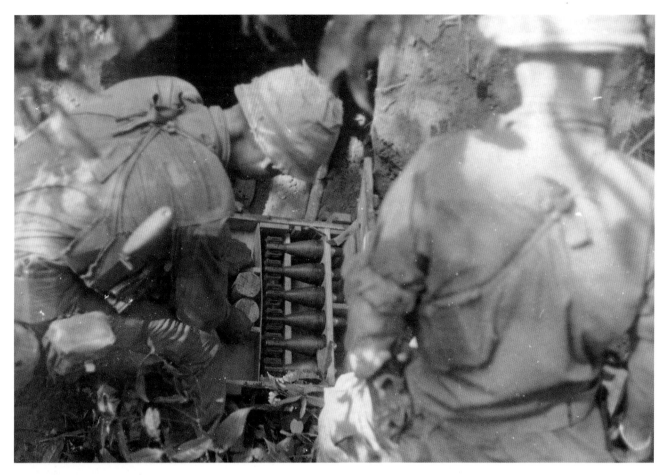

Two soldiers uncover a box of 82mm mortar rounds on Hill 1230 at the beginning of Operation MacArthur in the Central Highlands, November 1967.

An American soldier crouches behind a captured NVA DShK 12.7mm heavy machine gun. Developed by Russia during the Second World, the DShK was the NVA equivalent of the .50-caliber heavy machine gun. It has proven such a reliable and effective weapon that variants of it are still in use today around the world. June 1968.

A Marine fires an M2A1-7 flamethrower at a hut during Operation New Castle, March 26, 1967. The flamethrower could reach out to over 100 feet although its most effective range was under 70 feet.

A soldier holds a captured RPG-7 rocket launcher, among other enemy ammunition including grenades, bullets, and mortar rounds. Every weapon captured was one less the VC and NVA could use on the battlefield, but supplies continued to funnel south through the Ho Chi Minh Trail.

Members of U.S. Navy SEALs X-Ray Platoon. The SEAL in the center of the photo, Lt. Michael Collins, holds a Stoner 63 assault rifle, which fired a 5.56mm x 45mm cartridge. U.S. NAVY

A cache of Viet Cong weapons. The enemy were resourceful in using whatever they could find in order to arm and equip their cadre.

Sergeant Curtis E. Hester firing his M16 rifle while Sergeant Billy H. Faulks calls for air support for Company D, 151st (Ranger) Infantry, 1969. Hester is wearing an ERDL combat blouse while Faulks wears a Tigerstripe blouse. U.S. ARMY HERITAGE AND EDUCATION CENTER

Sgt. Adelbert F. Waldron III of the 6th Battalion, 31st Infantry Sniper, takes aim with his 7.62mm M21 sniper rifle, 1969. Sergeant Waldron had 109 confirmed kills to his credit, including a 900-meter kill of a Viet Cong sniper from a moving riverine boat on the Mekong River.

Examples of the U.S. Army XM21 (modified M14), a select-fire automatic rifle, with twenty-round external box magazine; and a USMC M40 (Remington 700) bolt-action rifle with five-round internal magazine.

The aftermath of battle. Dead Viet Cong are lined up beside their weapons, which include rocket-propelled grenades, AK-47s, and grenades. Counting weapons and bodies became an important way of measuring success against the elusive enemy.

A captured Czech-made copy of the Russian DShK heavy machine gun. Firing a 12.7mm shell, the DShK was equivalent to the American .50-caliber machine gun. October 1968.

Captured Viet Cong weapons, including RPG-7s and several DShK machine guns. November 1969.

A quad .50-caliber machine gun set up in a heavily sandbagged bunker. Originally designed as an antiaircraft weapon in World War II, the quad would prove very valuable in Vietnam against ground targets.

105mm shells peppered with shrapnel from North Vietnamese mortar rounds. June 1969.

A heavy forklift moves pallets of 155mm shells in an arms depot. May 1969.

The crew of a U.S. Army 155mm howitzer loading a round for a fire mission. Note the bunker in the background, its walls a mix of empty ammo crates and shell canisters.

A fantastic overhead shot of a firebase. Six 155mm guns are emplaced in sandbagged revetments and offer a 360-degree arc of fire for the base. May 1969.

Troops engage in maintenance of a 155mm howitzer named *Cong Crusher* in June 1969.

Sergeant Max Cones (gunner) fires an M107 175mm self-propelled gun of Battery C, 1st Battalion, 83rd Artillery, 54th Artillery Group, in 1968. With its 450-horsepower V8 engine, the M107 was capable of speeds up to 50 miles per hour on good roads. U.S. ARMY HERITAGE AND EDUCATION CENTER

Marines prepare to fire their 105mm gun from a forward fire base. Dating back to World War II, the M101A1 105mm gun proved a reliable infantry support weapon that was easily and quickly air transportable by helicopter to hilltop fire bases throughout South Vietnam.

A pair of U.S. Army 155mm howitzers set up in a fire support base. The 155 had a maximum range of 16,000 yards and could fire four rounds per minute when required.

The 155mm howitzer could fire any number of shells, including smoke and high explosive, with the weight of the shells varying between 90 and 100 pounds.

A soldier gingerly grabs an unexploded mortar shell that has landed near a 155mm ammunition bunker. Another unexploded shell is just to his right. Had either mortar shell hit and exploded among the 155mm shells, the resulting explosion would have been devastating. August 1969.

A close-up view of a 155mm howitzer named *Miss Mumqaard*. Note the heavy hydraulic jack beneath the gun, allowing it to be pivoted. August 1969.

At Le Than (1st Brigade headquarters), an 8-inch howitzer of the 5/16th Artillery fires against enemy positions. The gun is used as an offensive weapon and at the same time to support the infantry. Manning the number-three howitzer, named *Dante Jr.*, are 1st Sgt. Walter J. Rice, chief of section; Sgt. Raymond F. Shelburn, gunner; PFC David L. Classen, No. 1 man and loader/rammer; PFC Donnie Evans, No. 2 man and charger/firer; PFC Jimmy F. Tatom, assistant gunner; and Lt. Frederich R. Hackman, Delta Battery executive officer.

An M107 self-propelled howitzer 175mm (6.9-inch) gun at the moment of firing during Operation San Angelo, 1968. It had a maximum range of 21 miles and a crew of thirteen, which, when pressed, could fire one shell a minute. U.S. ARMY HERITAGE AND EDUCATION CENTER

CHAPTER 5
AVIATION

U.S. Army Bell UH-1D helicopters airlift members of the 2nd Battalion, 14th Infantry Regiment, from the Filhol Rubber Plantation area to a new staging area during Operation "Wahiawa," a search-and-destroy mission conducted by the 25th Infantry Division, northeast of Cu Chi, South Vietnam, 1966. USAF

Bell UH-1 Huey slicks come in to land. While its official name was Iroquois, the helicopter became known as Huey after its original designation of HU-1 (Helicopter Utility).

A row of UH-1 Hueys in their revetments. It became necessary to protect each aircraft as the Viet Cong and NVA would take every opportunity to mortar and rocket air fields and bases.

A UH-1 of the 174th Helicopter Assault Company (Dolphins and Sharks) is fueled up before a flight.

AH-1G Cobra gunship helicopter of the 334th Helicopter Company, 145th Aviation Battalion, photographed in Vietnam, 1969. Cobras entered service in 1968 and operated as attack platforms, aerial artillery, and hunter-killer teams with OH-6A Scout helicopters acting as spotters. U.S. ARMY HERITAGE AND EDUCATION CENTER

A Huey gunship mounting a pair of miniguns and a pair of 2.75-inch rocket pods of the 361st Pink Panthers, stationed at Pleiku Air Base, June 1968. This particular Huey was flown by Tim Dalbev. The Pink Panthers were assigned to provide aerial support to all operations in the II Corps area of Vietnam, which included missions into Laos and Cambodia.

Nose art proliferated during the war, and the Huey of Tim Dalbev of the 361st Aviation Company (Escort) Pink Panthers definitely got its share. In addition to the top hat–wearing Pink Panther on the nose, there is art labeled "The Hungry i" on each door, photographed at Pleiku.

The view out of the door gunner's position from a U.S. Marine Corps Sikorsky UH-34D Seahorse helicopter from Marine Medium Helicopter Transport Squadron 162 (HMM-162) over Vietnam, circa 1965. The gunner's M60 machine gun is in the foreground, with another UH-34D in the background.

This Green Hornet UH-1 of the 20th Special Operations Squadron takes on supplies at the forward operation location at Duc Lap, South Vietnam. It is hauling lumber and plywood sheets as part of the Pony Express, the secret missions flown in support of the equally secret radar sites in Laos.
U.S. AIR FORCE

Seen here mounted on a Huey is the XM 21 system with its M134 minigun capable of firing 4,000 rounds per minute. This was a scaled-down version of the M61 Vulcan 20mm cannon. The minigun is set over a seven-tube 2.75-inch rocket launcher XM 158 rocket pod. May 1968.

A crewman works on the minigun of a Huey of the 361st Aviation Company (Escort), May 1968.

Within the antipersonnel rockets were hundreds of 1.5-inch Flechettes, essentially small nails that would spread out like the blast from a shotgun.

A door gunner's view of Vietnam.

The M5 armament system was based on the M75 40mm belt-fed grenade launcher in a flexible, rotating ball turret. The launcher could fire up to 225 rounds per minute.

A forward view of the minigun and rocket-pod combination. If the enemy could be found, this lethal combination could spit out devastating fire.

Specialist E5 John Brennan, 114th Assault Helicopter Company (The Knights of the Air), Served in the Heart of the Mekong Delta at Vinh Long Army Air Field from March 17, 1970, to April 5, 1971

I flew a desk in Flight Operations for my tour.

The lift platoons were called the Red Knights and White Knights. The gun platoons were known as the Cobras and Lancers. For nine years the 114th called Vinh Long in IV Corps its home.

There were mortar attacks nearly every payday at night, the first of the month, and you could count the explosions as they walked across the airfield toward their intended targets. However, on August 5, 1970, the ammo dump exploded—which everyone around thought was some sort of VC secret weapon based on the seismic devastation it rendered. Noth-ing proved that point more clearly, and compounded the situation most directly, than the newly formed crater and the emergence of an enveloping cloud of CS gas (tear gas) that wafted across the compound seconds after the blast, wreaking havoc with all who encountered it.

On many an occasion, I was a passenger on a UH-1 Huey, always with cargo doors open and temperate winds ruffling everything inside. I inadvertently lost my 35mm camera's lens cap on one such flight. One other memorable flight was my last in-country Huey ride to the out-processing station at Long Bien. The pilot jok-ingly cut the power to the engine while in-flight to scare the unsuspecting DEROSing buddy on board as a final gesture of good-bye fun to a brother aviator who likewise was heading out of country on the stateside-bound Freedom Bird.

John Brennan standing in front of a stack of 2.75-inch folding-fin aerial rockets at Vinh Long Army Air Field, South Vietnam.

A seemingly less dangerous position to be—behind a desk—until the mortar rounds started falling, as they did every payday at Vinh Long, according to John Brennan.

Brennan beside a shark-mouthed Cobra attack helicopter with a full complement of rockets loaded.

Vietnam was beautiful, exotic, and dangerous. If not for the war, this country could be a great tourist destination. The people had deep wisdom and enduring patience. Their ability to maintain balance between their ancient culture and modern advances was a marvel.

I was asleep in my hotel room during my R&R stay in Sydney, Australia, when the phone rang and the voice on the other end was my girlfriend in California. Unlike today, that was unimaginable and the most unlikely thing to expect down-under back in January 1971. In 1992 I went back to the former site of the VLAAF. Nothing remains except the hangars.

A view of a HH-53 Jolly Giant helicopter of the 40th Aerospace Rescue and Recovery Squadron as seen from the gunner's position a helicopter of the 21st Special Operations Squadron, October 1972. U.S. AIR FORCE / KEN HACKMAN

Unofficial badge on coveralls belonging to Maj. Dean H. Williams Jr., who served in the USAF from 1942 to 1972. Major Williams served in the South Pacific during World War II and was stationed at Udorn Royal Thai Air Force Base and Nakhon Phanom Royal Thai Air Force Base during the war in Southeast Asia. He also flew special operations and Jolly Green helicopter rescue missions in Southeast Asia as well as participating in missions to Lima Site 85. U.S. AIR FORCE

By 1968, typical USAF combat rescue packages included strike aircraft, aerial refuelers, and rescue helicopters. U.S. AIR FORCE

A Boeing CH-47 Chinook of the 179th Assault Support Helicopter Company comes in to land at Camp Holloway, Pleiku. The Chinook was a true workhorse and often transported artillery pieces slung underneath the aircraft to forward operating bases. It would then make continuous flights to deliver munitions, food, and even reinforcements while often retrieving wounded and bringing them back. As a transport, the Chinook was lightly armed, usually with just a pair of M60 machine guns, one on each side of the aircraft. Just visible in the upper left of the photo is a Sikorsky CH-54 Tahre (nicknamed "The Crane"). It was designed to carry heavy loads, but was ultimately supplanted by the CH-47 Chinook.

The Marines' medium lift helicopter was the similar-looking Vertol CH-46 Sea Knight. The CH-46 in the photograph is part of HMM 364, a Marine Medium Helicopter Squadron known as the Purple Foxes. In addition to its many combat actions in South Vietnam, the Purple Foxes would be involved in the evacuation of the American embassy in Saigon.

An interesting shot showing three of the main helicopters used in the Vietnam War. In front is a UH-1 Huey, to the far right a CH-47 Chinook, and in the rear a CH-54 Sky Crane.

A Sikorsky CH-54 Tahre "Skycrane" prepares to lift a section of bridge. Able to lift up to 20,000 pounds, the Skycrane was nonetheless replaced by the CH-47 Chinook for heavy lift capabilities.

Major Reginald Hathorn, USAF, Call Sign "Nail 31," Forward Air Controller, June 1968 to June 1969

Major Reginald Hathorn with a combat photographer. DET 12. 601ST PHOTO FLIGHT

After one of his first combat sorties over Laos, Reg Hathorn fills out information in his maintenance logbook.

Major Hathorn's O-2, painted black for night missions. After two months and forty-two missions, it had bagged seventy-five trucks, five elephants, one helicopter, ten 37mm antiaircraft guns, two wide-beamed boats, and a motorcycle.

This A-1H Skyraider is fitted with the large propane bomb called "Fat Albert." It was designed for use against bunkers and underground tunnels.

Operating under the code name COMMANDO SABRE, FACs (forward air controllers) flying two-seat F-100F Super Sabres armed with white phosphorous rockets to mark enemy positions for follow-on aircraft to bomb began replacing slower, propeller-driven FACs in areas where enemy antiaircraft artillery fire was heavy. These fast FACs became known as Misty after their call sign. The first Misty flight began in June 1967 and quickly grew in scope to cover infiltration points of the Ho Chi Minh Trail as well as areas in Laos and North Vietnam. U.S. AIR FORCE

A formation of Cessna A-37Bs of the 757th Special Operations Group. Called the Dragonfly or Super Tweet, the A-37B operated in a close-support role, in addition to FAC and night interdiction missions. The A-37B design was spurred by the need for counterinsurgency aircraft. Ultimately, the majority of A-37Bs served with the South Vietnamese Air Force. U.S. AIR FORCE

A Cessna A-37B (S/N 68-10803) of the VNAF flying out of Da Nang Air Base. In addition to hard points to carry bombs, rocket pods, and fuel tanks, the A-37B was armed with a 7.62mm minigun in its nose. U.S. AIR FORCE

Gunships provided crucial close air support for nighttime defense of hamlets, outposts, and military bases. The top photo shows shows an AC-119G from the 17th Special Operations Squadron from Nha Trang Air Base over Tan Son Nhut Air Base in 1969. The second and third photo show AC-119G "Shadow" gunners preparing for a mission and the interior of the cargo compartment equipped with its four SUU-11B/A 7.62 miniguns. U.S. AIR FORCE

An AC-130A Spooky (also called Spectre) gunship at Ubon Royal Thai Air Force Base in the spring of 1969. As the name implies, the aircraft was a flying gun platform and carried four 20mm cannons and four 7.62mm miniguns. U.S. AIR FORCE

Here is another adaption made to the C-130 Hercules with a "Black Crow" sensor on *Thor*, an AC-130A gunship. This sensor detected and tracked vehicles by the electrical impulses of their spark plugs. *Thor* was shot down by antiaircraft fire in December 1972, with the loss of fourteen of its sixteen crew. U.S. AIR FORCE

A C-130E Hercules of the 346th Tactical Airlift Squadron (tail code DY) of the 314th Troop Carrier Wing, stationed at Ching Chuan Kang Air Base, Taiwan, May 1969. The E was an improved version of the B model, with the addition of two 1,360-gallon external fuel tanks, improved turboprop engines, and upgraded avionics.

A flight of four Operation Ranch Hand aircraft spray the defoliant Agent Orange over the jungle in South Vietnam. Designed to kill crops and deny the enemy cover, the toxic mix of chemicals is also considered by many to have contributed to long term illnesses in veterans, including multiple forms of cancer.

Aircraft spraying defoliant agent over the jungle while a fighter, possibly an F-105, provides cover. Operation Ranch Hand ran from 1961 to 1971 and used the now infamous herbicide and defoliant mixture known as Agent Orange. It was believed that destroying large swathes of jungle would prevent the Viet Cong from hiding and destroy the food crops they relied on.

Senior Airman Jim Haley, USAF, 305th OMS (Organizational Maintenance Squadron), KC-135 Mechanic Stationed at U-Tapao Air Base, Thailand, and Kadena Air Base, Okinawa, August 1972 to August 1973

I flew "Looking Glasses" as well as "Radio Relay" and normal tankers but also flew in the KC-135Q. The Q model was designed specifically to fuel SR-71 Blackbirds, which used a special JP7 low-ignition fuel due to the extreme heat that built up in the aircraft when flying at a high cruising speed. The "Radio Relay" flights were necessary to assist U.S. Navy carrier-based aircraft whose radios had too short of a range, making the relay necessary. Because of high flight tempos, a "Radio Relay" aircraft was in orbit twenty-four hours a day.

USAF Senior Airman Jim Haley, 1971.

A Lockheed U2 spy plane of the 99th Strategic Reconnaissance Squadron parked behind a B-52 bomber on U-Tapao Air Base. The U2 was designed as a high-altitude reconnaissance aircraft and was first deployed flying missions for the Central Intelligence Agency before the Air Force also began flying the aircraft.

Another Lockheed U2 spy plane of the 99th SRS being prepped for flight at U-Tapao Air Base, 1971. Only one U2 was lost during combat operations, and that was due to mechanical difficulties over North Vietnam. The pilot was able to bring his plane back over friendly ground and safely eject.

A Ryan Aeronautical 147 Lightning Bug drone hangs from its pylon on the wing of a C-130 aircraft at U-Tapao. During the course of the war, Ryan would produce thousands of Model 147 drones in a myriad of variants, with the main focus being reconnaissance at both low and high altitude. The Lightning Bug was based on the Firebee target drone, which was converted to conduct ever more complicated reconnaissance missions with the fitting of cameras, larger wings, bigger fuel tanks, and increasingly sophisticated electronics.

A Boeing B-52 Stratofortress bomber barrels down the runway on takeoff. Known by the acronym BUFF—Big Ugly Fat Fucker—the B-52 was designed as a nuclear bomber, but adapted well to carrying conventional bombs. First flown in 1952, the eight-engine bomber was progressively upgraded during the war. The D model with the "Big Belly" modification could carry a staggering eighty 500-pound bombs and an additional twenty-four 500-pound bombs externally under the wings. JIM HALEY

A U.S. Air Force Boeing B-52D-35-BW Stratofortress (s/n 52-669) dropping bombs over Vietnam. This aircraft was hit by an SA-2 surface-to-air missile over North Vietnam during the Linebacker II offensive on 31 December 1972 and crashed in Laos. The crew of six ejected, but only five were rescued. USAF

Three F-105D Thunderchiefs (Thuds) roll down the runway on a bombing mission in North
Vietnam. Designed as an all-weather attack fighter, the Thud was capable of flying Mach 2 at high
altitude although it would fly most of its missions in Vietnam at lower altitudes. Its role as a fighter-
bomber would eventually be taken over by the F4 Phantom. U.S. AIR FORCE

Of the 143 F-105F trainers built, 86 were converted into Wild Weasels like the one pictured here.
The Wild Weasel mission was an exceptionally dangerous one that involved flying ahead of strike
packages to entice SAM sites to turn on their radar. Carrying radar that could pinpoint the SAM
radar, the Wild Weasel aircraft would fire an AGM-54 Shrike missile, which would home in on the
SAM radar and, hopefully, destroy it. U.S. AIR FORCE

An F4 Phantom comes up to an aerial tanker for refueling during Operation Rolling Thunder, the three-year bombing campaign from 1965 to 1968 against North Vietnam. Aerial refueling gave aircraft such as the Phantom the range to operate in the northern part of North Vietnam.
U.S. AIR FORCE

469th Tactical Fighter Squadron pilots: Capt. Bruce Holmes, Capt. Will Koenitzer, and Capt. William "Bart" Barthelmas. Barthelmas was killed in action on July 27, 1965, on the first U.S. Air Force airstrike against North Vietnamese surface-to-air missile sites.
U.S. AIR FORCE

The charred hulk of a USAF McDonnell Douglass F4 II Phantom. This was one of 445 USAF Phantoms lost during the war. Of those, 382 went down in combat, most to ground fire from AAA and SAMs.

Colonel Robin Olds, commander of the 8th Tactical Fighter Wing at Ubon Air Base, Thailand. A World War II fighter ace, Olds added four North Vietnamese MiGs to his tally. He is seen here in front of *Scat XXVII*, keeping up the tradition of naming all his aircraft after a former roommate at flight school. U.S. AIR FORCE

RF-4C pilot Capt. Robert Clark being congratulated after finishing his second 100-mission RF-4C tour. The "2 to go" on his aircraft represented his wish to fly two more 100-mission tours. He later flew missions as a B-52G pilot over North Vietnam during Linebacker II. U.S. AIR FORCE

A Wild Weasel crew of the 44th Tactical Fighter Squadron of the 388th Tactical Fighter Wing pose beside their F-105F Thud. U.S. AIR FORCE

A photograph of Wolf FACs of 8th Tactical Fighter Wing Ubon Royal Thai AB in June 1968. Drawn from the four squadrons assigned to the wing, these pilots volunteered for the Fast FAC missions. The F-4 is from the 497th Tactical Fighter Squadron, and the squadron's "Night Owl" symbol is just behind the air inlet. U.S. AIR FORCE

Staff Sgt. Alexander Underwood, a B-66 flight engineer, completed his 100th mission over North Vietnam on September 21, 1966. On the mission, while flying over the North, Underwood took his reenlistment oath. U.S. AIR FORCE

Col. (later Maj. Gen.) Robert Maloy (left) and Capt. William S. Paul (right) of the 366th Tactical Fighter Wing after being rescued by an H-3E Jolly Green Giant from the 37th Aerospace Rescue and Recovery Squadron on October 15, 1967. Enemy fire hit their F-4 Phantom over North Vietnam, but they reached open water before ejecting. Maloy fractured his back, and Pararescueman (PJ) Airman 1st Class Roger Klenovich (center, wearing red PJ beret) went into the water to help. U.S. AIR FORCE

F-4 Phantom II pilot Capt. Mike McCarthy and his rear-seater, Marcus Hurley, about to take off on one of the first AGM-62 Walleye TV-guided weapon missions (the Walleye is the white object to the far right in the photo). McCarthy and Hurley flew for the 433rd Tactical Fighter Squadron, Satan's Angels. McCarthy would earn the Distinguished Flying Cross for completing 124 combat missions in the air war over North Vietnam as well as Laos. MIKE MCCARTHY

This Martin RB-57E was named *Patricia Lynn* and painted in low observable black while stationed at Da Nang Air Base, South Vietnam, in January 1964. The bomber was converted to carry cameras and served in aerial reconnaissance units. This aircraft was lost on October 25, 1968. U.S. AIR FORCE

A McDonnell RF-101C on a photo-reconnaissance flight over Vietnam in May 1967. Although originally designed as a strike fighter capable of carrying a nuclear bomb, the VooDoo would see combat as a reconnaissance platform until being supplanted by the F-4 Phantom. U.S. AIR FORCE

A Curtiss C-46 Commando twin-engine airplane operated by Air America, a front for the Central Intelligence Agency, in Vietnam. Originally launched in 1950, Air America flew many covert operations before and during American involvement in the Vietnam War. With a mixed fleet of helicopters and propeller-driven aircraft, Air America flew supplies—everything from rice and water buffaloes to arms and ammunition—as well as passengers ranging from spies, refugees, commandos, diplomats, and senior politicians. It was also involved in drug smuggling, although the CIA denies that it sanctioned such activity.

Self-portrait of the copilot of a UH-1 Huey helicopter. Flying a helicopter requires both hands, the right on the control and the left on the collective, so it seems likely this was the copilot snapping a photo while in flight. Troops took cameras with them in all theaters of operations; many of these photos are published in this book.

A North Vietnamese Mikoyan-Gurevich MiG-17 is hit by 20mm shells from a U.S. Air Force Republic F-105D Thunderchief piloted by Maj. Ralph Kuster Jr. from the 469th Tactical Fighter Squadron, 388th Tactical Figther Wing, on June 3, 1967. U.S. AIR FORCE

A pair of PBRs (patrol boat, river) surround a South Vietnamese sampan. Weapons and supplies were smuggled along rivers in sampans, making it imperative that the boats be inspected for contraband.

A PBR in a patriotic shot on a river in South Vietnam. As part of the Brown River Navy, the PBR patrolled the waterways of Vietnam and was made even more famous in the movie *Apocalypse Now*. With its fiberglass hull, the PBR was fast, but offered little protection from enemy fire. Ceramic armor shields were affixed to the guns and bridge as a way to mitigate this. The PBR was typically armed with a twin .50-caliber machine gun in the front, a single .50-caliber in the rear, an M60 machine gun, and an Mk19 grenade launcher.

Vietnamese plied the waterways in all number of craft, making the job of interdicting weapons and ammunition coming down from the North very challenging.

A portable firing platform with a 105mm howitzer on deck. Riverine warfare required new and innovative means to bring fire to bear on the enemy. Without firm ground to set up an artillery fire base, the portable firing platform was used. It had four adjustable legs with large "feet" that rested on the bottom of the river or rice paddy to provide a stable firing platform. The artillery, ammunition, platform, and crew were airlifted into position by helicopters.

A river monitor cruises down the river like a battleship on the high seas, although it started life as a World War II landing craft before being heavily converted. The turret in the bow of the boat houses a 40mm gun.

An Armored Troop Carrier (ATC) in all its ungainly beauty. Able to transport a fully equipped platoon of forty men and all their gear, the ATC provided significant protection from enemy small-arms fire. The slatted walls covering the ATC were designed to detonate RPG rounds before they could penetrate the boat. U.S. ARMY

A command-and-control boat based on the river monitor hull.

Another converted landing craft, the ATC (armored troop carrier) was known as a Tango boat. With added armor up 2.5 inches thick and bristling with weapons, the Tangos could carry a full platoon of forty men in relative safety.

A pair of U.S. Navy patrol craft, fast (PCF), better known as swift boats, on patrol. Their swiftness was due in part to their light aluminum hulls.

Fast patrol craft PCF-38 of Coastal Division 11 patrols the Cai Ngay Canal in South Vietnam, April 1970.

A PAC-V (patrol air cushioned vehicle). Suspected Viet Cong are led off a "Pac Vee" hovercraft to interrogation. Only a handful of these vehicles were used during the Vietnam War.

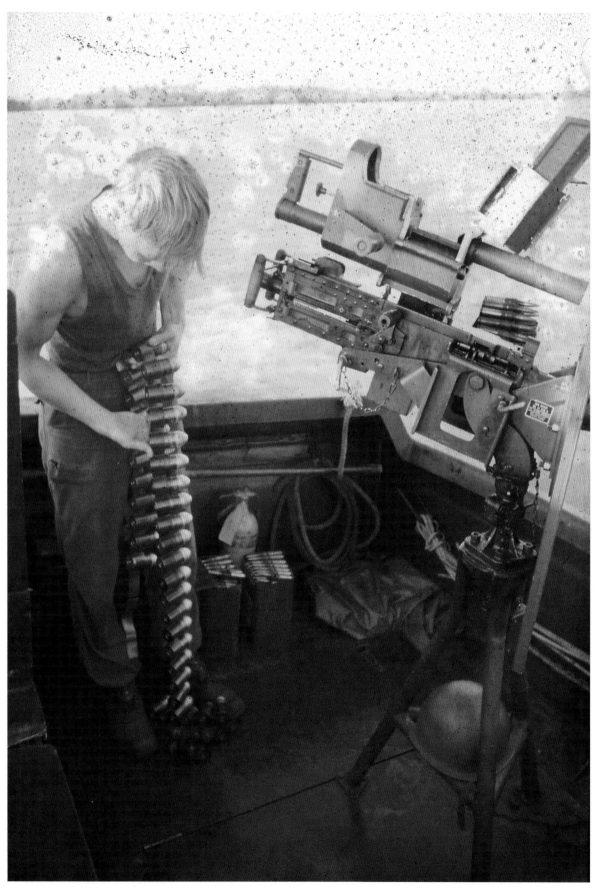

A sailor onboard a PBR loads a Mk19 40mm grenade launcher. The Mk19 had a range of over 2,000 yards and was fully automatic.

An ASPB (assault support patrol boat). This was a purpose-built design for riverine warfare and was used to conduct night operations and patrols. Its exhaust system vented under the water line, making it very quiet. It was typically armed with a single 20mm canon as well as a twin. 50-caliber machine gun. It could also carry an 81mm mortar.

Not as well known, the U.S. Coast Guard served in Vietnam. As part of Operation Market Time, they patrolled the coastal shores of South Vietnam to interdict supplies and weapons being shipped from the North. Division 12 of Coast Guard Squadron One arrived in DaNang on 20 July 1965. Division 11 of USCG Squadron One deployed to An Thoi, arriving on 31 July 1965. Division 13 of USCG Squadron One deployed to Cat Lo, arriving on 22 February 1966. Additional units were added, including Squadron Three, which began patrolling on 15 May 1967 with five high-endurance cutters. On May 5, 1973, the last USCG personnel left South Vietnam. This ship was photographed in December 1968.

U.S. Navy SEALs with a captured B-40 (North Vietnamese licensed copy of the RPG-7). The SEALs were tasked with antiguerrilla warfare and were also part of the CIA's Phoenix Program, the assassination of high-level Viet Cong and North Vietnamese Army operatives. The first SEALs deployed to Vietnam in March 1962. Their operations would eventually take them into North Vietnam, Laos, and Cambodia as well.

The USS *Colleton* began life as a barracks ship, its keel being laid in June 1945 toward the end of World War II. After an extensive refit, the ship provided expanded medical treatment and casualty-holding facilities for the Mobile Riverine Force during the Tet Offensive. Despite not having a full-time surgeon on board, the *Colleton* served ably as a hospital ship, providing emergency lifesaving treatment and stabilization before the casualties were transported to larger medical facilities.

Aircraft burning aboard the U.S. Navy nuclear-powered aircraft carrier USS *Enterprise* (CVAN-65), January 14, 1969. The fire started when a Zuni rocket accidentally exploded under the wing of an F-4J Phantom II off Hawaii. The following explosions blew holes in the flight deck and killed 28 people, wounding 343; fifteen aircraft were destroyed. U.S. NAVY

A U.S. Navy Douglas A-4F Skyhawk of Attack Squadron VA-212 (Rampant Raiders) passes by a landing signal officer (LSO) on its way to trapping on board the aircraft carrier USS *Hancock* (CVA-19) off Vietnam, May 21, 1972. VA-212 was assigned to Carrier Air Wing 21 (CVW-21) aboard the *Hancock* for a deployment to Vietnam from January 7 to October 3, 1972.

Two U.S. Navy F-4B-14-MC Phantom II (BuNo 150482, 150485) from Fighter Squadron VF-41 (Black Aces) launching from the aircraft carrier USS *Independence* (CVA-62) for a strike in Vietnam. VF-41 was assigned to Carrier Air Wing 7 (CVW-7) aboard the *Independence* for a deployment to Vietnam from May 10 to December 13, 1965.

A pair of U.S. Navy Attack Squadron 85 (VA-85) A-6A intruder attack aircraft in flight over the South China Sea with their tailhooks extended for recovery aboard the attack aircraft carrier USS *Kitty Hawk* (CVA-63), January 1966. The two-seat Grumman A-6A Intruder served as both the Navy's and Marines' primary medium, all-weather attack aircraft throughout the war. It was able to carry a bomb load of up to 18,000 pounds, more than twice the bomb load typically carried by a four-engine B-17 bomber in World War II.

In addition to their wartime duties, several carriers like the *Essex*-class USS *Hornet* also served as recovery platforms for the Apollo Moon Missions during the Vietnam War. In this photo from July 1969, President Richard M. Nixon welcomes the crew of Apollo 11 back from their successful mission to walk on the moon. Safely ensconced in their quarantine facility, Neil A. Armstrong (commander), Michael Collins (command module pilot), and Edwin E. "Buzz" Aldrin Jr. (lunar module pilot) look out at President Nixon. The *Hornet* would undertake three Vietnam cruises during the war.

With the impending fall of Saigon and the defeat of South Vietnam by the North, South Vietnamese fearing for their lives took every possible means of transportation to flee. Here a South Vietnamese UH-1H is pushed overboard after landing on an American carrier to make way for more aircraft coming in to land.

CHAPTER 7
VEHICLES

The M113 armored personnel carrier was the standard American infantry ground transport in combat operations during the Vietnam War. Featuring aluminum armor to keep its weight down, the M113 could travel at speeds up to 40 miles per hour over flat ground. This particular carrier has been equipped with a turret for an M2 .50-caliber machine gun as well as a shield for an M60 machine gun.

Specialist 4th Class Jim Ross, U.S. Army, Company A, 2nd Battalion, 22nd Infantry (Mechanized), 25th Infantry Division (25 February–22 November 1970); Company A, 1st Battalion, 8th Cavalry, 1st Cavalry Division (Airmobile) (23 November–5 February 1971)

I was a twenty-year-old with almost two years of college when drafted in July 1969. My time with the 25th "Tropic Lightning" Division was spent in the vicinity of Cu Chi (near the Iron Triangle), which was northwest of Saigon. I was in a mechanized battalion (the "Triple Deuce") and served primarily as a rifleman and machine-gunner, but at times also wore the hats of demolitions man and tunnel rat. Our unit spent thirty-eight days in Cambodia during the May–June 1970 incursion to clear NVA base camps there. When the 25th redeployed to Hawaii in November, I was transferred to the 1st Cavalry Division as a straight-leg grunt. Brigade HQ was at Song Be, but our battalion operated out of LZ Dragonhead in the mountainous jungle to the southeast.

This shot was taken by a squad mate of Jim Ross, Dennis "Ranger" Hiedeman, as their APC crossed the Rach Cai Bach River into Cambodia via a temporary pontoon bridge on 7 May 1970. The point of crossing was northwest of Tay Ninh at the lower end of the border area they called the Dog's Face. At the time, Ross was a rifleman and had a seat on an ammo box on the right rear deck of the track.

Rottin 8 No. 2 at LZ Devin. This fire support base was located just outside the village of Go Dau Ha on Highway 1, about thirty miles northwest of Cu Chi. The photo is one of those almost obligatory "dress up" pictures that all grunts (kids) posed for at one time or another. Seated atop the track is driver John Keinroth. Standing, left to right: Dennis "Ranger" Hiedeman, unknown (possibly Vernon Glenn), and Jim Ross.

I knew little about the war going in, other than we were supposed to help keep the South Vietnamese free from communism. In spite of the protests, I thought it was my duty to serve when called, and I did so proudly. Had the U.S. prosecuted the war differently, we may have prevailed, though how long the South might have stayed free with the political corruption there is another question. I was exceptionally lucky to come home in one piece. Even now, thinking of some of the "near misses" causes me to shudder. Like all combat veterans, I've wondered why I made it when others didn't. Obviously, there is no answer. We simply have to accept it and continue on.

As challenging as it was, I believe that the majority of the troops performed their jobs honorably. Certainly, each soldier's experience was unique. I know that many fellow veterans have carried the burden of mental or physical scars ever since. I can't speak for others, but in my case it seems a small price to pay compared to how bad it could have been.

A Zippo at work. Flame tracks were used periodically during search-and-destroy missions to scorch bunker complexes and tunnels and to clear ground cover. This one is working out in an area of tall elephant grass in the Filhol area of operations northeast of 25th Infantry Division HQ at Cu Chi base camp in March or April 1970.

An NVA prisoner taken on Ambush Alley. This photo was taken by Jim Ross during the Cambodian incursion when he was a .50 gunner. Ross believes it was a simple case of the NVA walking out of the woods with hands up in surrender during a rest stop. This soldier is a textbook, well-outfitted, standard-issue North Vietnamese Regular, with pith helmet, khaki pants, OD green shirt, and Ho Chi Minh sandals.

A rare modification to a M151 Mutt by the personnel of the
Naval Communications Station at U.S. Navy Base Cam
Ranh Bay, turning it into a one of a kind Dune Buggy.
Commander William J. Longhi stands beside the creative
vehicle, named *Bad News.* 1970–71. U.S. NAVAL HISTORY AND
HERITAGE COMMAND / WILLIAM J. LONGHI

An M88 armored recovery vehicle hoists an M113 armored personnel carrier
onto a flatbed truck. Recovery of armored vehicles in Vietnam proved
challenging because of the lack of paved roads and the difficult terrain the
vehicles often operated in.

Marine and Army 2½-ton trucks hit in several places by mortar fragments. The trucks were built unarmored, but troops began to heavily modify them to protect against shrapnel, mines, and rocket-propelled grenades. August 1969.

Pictured here is an M-274 Mule armed with an M40 106mm recoilless rifle. The Mule had a top speed of 25 miles per hour, featured four-wheel drive, was built to handle rugged terrain, and was easily transported by helicopter. At least one Marine detachment in Vietnam mounted Xenon searchlights on Mules. CPL. J. L. MARTINEZ

An M48 tank with a mine roller attachment prepares to clear Highway 19 in South Vietnam. The danger of mines was ever present in Vietnam, and to combat the threat, experiments such as the mine roller were tried. The 11th Cavalry fitted a single M48 tank with a mine roller and tested it for eighty kilometers without finding a single mine. Ultimately, twenty-seven of the devices were used in Vietnam.

An armored unit picking up supplies that have been airlifted in by helicopter (note the pallet of boxes in the center of the photo) at Loc Ninh, November 1968.

A nice close-up of an M113 crewman wearing the composite-material helmet designed for use in armored vehicles. Unlike the M1 helmet used by soldiers and Marines, the armor crewman helmet was made of ballistic nylon and fiberglass. This photo was taken immediately after a firefight at Loc Ninh in November 1968.

A column of M113s pauses as a Rome Plow (vehicle to the far right) clears the ground for the night defensive position (NDP). The Rome Plows were armored bulldozers and got their name from their place of manufacture, Rome, Georgia.

A better view of the working end of a Rome Plow. Vehicles like these were indispensible in allowing armored vehicles like the M113 and M48 tank to move through the jungle terrain of South Vietnam.

M113s sweep down the lanes between trees on an old French plantation near Loc Ninh, November 1968.

M113 armored personnel carriers rumble over jungle vegetation in order to clear an area for a temporary laager and prevent the enemy from using the vegetation as camouflage.

M113 en route to village Seal, southwest of Anloc, December 1968.

A pair of USMC LVTP-5s (landing vehicle, tracked, personnel) in the sand. The LVTP-5 was designed to give Marines a lightly armored amphibious assault vehicle to ferry Marines ashore. It could carry a platoon of Marines along with a three-man crew.

Just one of thousands of construction sites that popped up all over Vietnam as the U.S. moved into areas and built bases, roads, bridges, and airfields. In the foreground, a heavily sandbagged watchtower/bunker provides protection over the encampment.

A supply convoy with lumber and a heavy road roller on the side of the road. The lack of infrastructure outside the cities meant U.S. forces had to build everything they needed, which meant bringing all the supplies along with them.

A road grader smooths out a section of road that had become rutted from heavy traffic, December 1967. Periodically grating the road also made it easier to spot mines laid by the Viet Cong.

A North Vietnamese Type 63 self-propelled antiaircraft gun destroyed by a 500-pound aerial bomb during the siege of An Loc during the North's Easter Offensive in 1972. The Type 63 was based on a Chinese copy of the T-34/85 tank with a new, open turret containing two 37mm antiaircraft guns.

U.S. AIR FORCE

M113s fording a stream in the jungle west of An Loc near the Cambodian border. In 1972 this area would become a bloody battlefield as the North Vietnamese invaded South Vietnam.

An M577 armored command vehicle of the 11th Armored Cavalry Regiment (the Blackhorse Regiment) rolls along, April 1969. Based on the M113 chassis, the M577 operated as a mobile command post equipped with radios and its own electric generator.

An Army 11th ACR M548 cargo carrier in Vietnam, April 1969. The carrier is an unarmored variant of the M113 carrier and features an open top. Behind the carrier is an M109 Paladin, a self-propelled 155mm howitzer.

Part of the same convoy, an 11th ACR M48 armored vehicle launched bridge in Vietnam. Of note is the emblazoned shield of the Blackhorse. Immediately behind the M48 AVLR is an M48 tank.

A row of M48 tanks, February 1968. With little enemy armor to contend with, the M48 operated in support of infantry operations throughout Vietnam.

A Marine Ontos crew member relaxes during a break in the fighting at Hue during the Tet Offensive, February 23, 1968. The Ontos—known officially as the rifle, multiple 106 mm, self-propelled M50—was a light tracked vehicle mounting six 106mm recoilless rifles. Designed as an antitank platform, the Ontos performed well against enemy infantry formations.
U.S. MARINE CORPS

An Army captain jokes around a USMC M48A3 Patton tank. With a top speed of 30 miles per hour, a 90mm main gun, and .50- and .30-caliber machine guns, the M48 was a useful tank for the difficult terrain of Vietnam. Ammunition for the main gun included high explosive, white phosphorous, canister (which was essentially a massive shotgun shell filled with steel pellets), and antitank rounds. The M48 proved to be a popular tank and was exported to numerous countries around the globe, including Pakistan and Israel, where it would prove itself again in more combat.

The M48 closest to the camera has "Good Bye Charley" painted on its barrel and a peace sign drawn over the cover of its Xenon searchlight—a mixed message, to be sure. February 1970.

M42 40mm self-propelled antiaircraft gun, nicknamed "Duster," pictured in September 1967. Originally sent to Vietnam to provide air defense, the Duster gradually took on more and more ground-support missions, in which its twin fully automatic 40mm Bofors guns excelled against enemy ground forces.

A trio of USAF Base Security V-100 armored personnel carriers, with the lead vehicle modified to carry a searchlight. All three are armed with mounted M-60 machine guns. U.S. AIR FORCE

A U.S. Army M706 Cadillac Gage Commando amphibious armored car, April 1969. Of note is the Confederate flag. With a top speed over 60 miles per hour and great all-round mobility, the M706 was ideal for convoy duty and base defense.

A view of a rare LeTourneau tree-crusher moving through the jungle. The 1st Logistical Command wanted something that could traverse the dense terrain and rented this vehicle from the United States on a trial basis. Though it performed well, it was deemed not reliable enough for use and was ultimately returned to the U.S. 1967.

A mixed armor package of M551 Sheridan tanks and M113 APCs, February 1969. The M551 was a light tank designed to be air portable. Its main gun was a hybrid 152mm that fired both conventional shells and the Shillelagh guided antitank missile. With its light, aluminum armor, the Sheridan suffered heavy casualties from rocket-propelled grenades and mines.

CHAPTER 8
VIETNAM

A South Vietnamese farmer and his son plow their rice field with a team of water buffalo. Rice was the main staple of the peoples' diet, and control of the rice crop was fiercely fought over.

During ceremonies at Saigon, South
Vietnam, in March, 1962, the Vietnamese
Air Force pledges its support for President
Ngo Dinh Diem after a political uprising
and an attempt on the president's life.
Diem became the first president of South
Vietnam in 1955 with the withdrawal of
French troops. His anticommunist fervor
drew strong support from the U.S., but his
oppression of the Montangard natives and
Buddhists stirred horrific protests in which
monks immolated themselves. Diem
eventually lost the backing of the U.S. and
was assassinated on November 3, 1963.
U.S. ARMY

A view of Nguyen Hue Circle in Saigon, South Vietnam, April 1969.

American culture, from soft drinks to movies, permeated South Vietnam during the war.

A common view from an American helicopter flying over the South Vietnamese landscape. The lush green patches are rice paddies getting close to harvest while the brown ones are paddies currently laying fallow. Traversing rice paddies meant walking through sometimes waist-high water of muck and manure. The alternative was walking along the berms that contained the water in each paddy, but doing so exposed the troops to enemy fire.

Aerial view of Saigon from 3,000 feet, July 1968.

Vietnamese army personnel training in the jungle, May 1962. Trained by U.S. advisors and equipped with U.S. equipment, many ARVN units fought bravely during the conflict although others lacked motivation and adequate leadership.

MACV (Military Assistance Command, Vietnam) I Corps Zone billets, Da Nang, December 1968.

These young men, from all of South Vietnam's forty-four provinces, will return to their native villages after thirteen weeks of training at the National Training Center. Their job: to help villagers help themselves. Circa 1970.

A view of MACV HQ in Saigon, June 1968.

A young soldier from the Popular Forces stands gate guard duty in Vietnam, 1968. Acting initially as a civil guard, these soldiers were recruited to protect their own villages from Viet Cong attack. In 1969 these units began being deployed outside their home districts as American force levels began falling.

A Vietnamese woman carrying two sacks of rice along the road, December 1967. Without stopping and searching her, American troops couldn't know if the bags contained only rice or ammunition, weapons, or some other supplies for the Viet Cong.

South Vietnamese women work in a rice field, September 1967. Clad in common dress of black or white blouses and pants and wearing conical straw hats, it was virtually impossible to tell which worker was really a farmer and which was Viet Cong. The reality was that many were both.

A street cleaner with her cart in South Vietnam. Much of the country lived in poverty, and many resorted to living off the scrap and refuse discarded by American forces.

A group of South Vietnamese children gather around, no doubt hoping for gifts of candy and other items from American soldiers, December 1967.

A group of South Vietnamese children play on a domesticated water buffalo, September 1967.

A My Tho–Saigon bus, September 1968. Located forty miles south of Saigon in the Mekong Delta, My Tho would witness heavy fighting during the Tet offensive, launched by the Viet Cong on 30 January 30 1968. Attacked by Viet Cong battalions 261st, 263rd, and 514th on 31 January, fighting raged in My Tho until 2 February, when elements of the U.S. Mobile Riverine Force and ARVN cleared the city by a combination of air assaults using napalm, artillery, and infantry attacks.

A bus servicing towns in South Vietnam. Fire Support Base Scott was built in an area known as Tan Tru and manned by elements of the 9th Infantry Division. The 2nd Brigade of the 9th often worked in conjunction with the Mobile Riverine Force, being deployed throughout the Mekong Delta.

An antimortar radar station and communications relay at Vung Tau, a coastal city to the east of Saigon. The radar was able to detect a mortar bomb in flight and then calculate where it had originated based on the bomb's parabolic flight profile. Vung Tau was a popular R&R city for troops who remained in-country for their leave.

A pair of ARVN soldiers poses for the camera. Trained and equipped by the United States, the ARVN (also known as the South Vietnamese Army, or SVA) would fight alongside American units throughout the war.

A South Vietnamese Air Force (VNAF) AC-47 gunship. In the late 1960s, the USAF turned over its AC-47s to the South Vietnamese and Royal Laotian Air Forces.

U.S. AIR FORCE

A Vietnamese soldier toasts the camera while American soldiers look on. The Vietnamese soldier wears tiger-stripe camo and is likely a Kit Carson scout, a former Viet Cong or North Vietnamese soldier who has defected and now serves the American army. First implemented by the Marines, the Kit Carson program expanded across Vietnam as General Westmoreland dictated that units employ the scouts in their effort to fight the Viet Cong.

The war took a heavy toll on the Vietnamese population, with an estimated 250,000 to 500,000 South Vietnamese civilians being killed during the conflict. For the wounded, the health services available were meager. To deal with the casualties, international help was provided through agencies like the Red Cross. Germany sent the hospital ship *Helgoland* to South Vietnam, where it stayed from the fall of 1966 until 1972. Docked at Saigon and then Da Nang, the *Helgoland*'s medical staff treated tens of thousands of civilians before finally sailing back to Germany as American forces withdrew. The writing on the van in the foreground says "Federal Republic of Germany Red Cross" in German, French, and Vietnamese.

CHAPTER 9

R&R AND GOING HOME

Entertainer Bob Hope tees off on the flight deck of the aircraft carrier USS *Ticonderoga* (CVA 14) during his visit off the coast of Vietnam on December 26, 1965. Hope and other entertainers were on a Christmas tour of American military installations throughout Vietnam. Hope became ubiquitous as an entertainer to the troops and traveled to Vietnam numerous times during the war. His extraordinary service to the troops was recognized with the naming of the USN *Bob Hope*, a vehicle cargo ship, after the performer. U.S. NAVY

A cigarette girl at a bar in Sydney, Australia, 1970. R&R outside Vietnam was much sought after, and Australia was a popular destination.

A sign warning Americans on leave in the Philippines. Fun was going to be had, but it was hoped that it would remain safe and contained. Unsurprisingly, that didn't always happen.

Darwin, Australia, was a stopping point along the R&R flight that took servicemen and women in Vietnam to Sydney. A week's R&R in Australia was a welcome change from a combat tour and offered many entertainment choices, from the mundane to the exotic.

Entertainment for the troops often focused on music and pretty women.

There were other, more personal,
forms of entertainment for the troops.

A soldier's decorated bunk area showing three of the main thoughts—peace, women, and a calendar marking down the days of his tour before he flew back to the World.

This soldier's sleeping quarters make it clear where his imagination liked to wander.

With the invention of portable tape players and recorders, soldiers could listen to music and record messages to loved ones back home. June 1969.

Captain Rodney Bothelo, 1st Shore Party Battalion, and Miss Elli Vade Bon Cowur, associate director of the USO, judges for the USO-sponsored surfing contest held September 25, 1966. They are shown with PFC Robert D. Binkley, FLSG-B, who took first place in the event; Cpl. Tim A. Crowder, Communications Company, Headquarters Battalion, second-place winner; and Lance Cpl. Steven C. Richardson, 1st Medical Battalion, third-place winner.

Thousands of service personnel listen to Miss Ann Margret sing one of her numbers during her show in Danang, Vietnam, March 13, 1966.

Roy and Dale Rogers entertain crew members of an Air Force C-123 Provider during the last leg of their Vietnam tour, November 1966. Crew members are (left to right) Airman Second Class Cyril F. Crawly, 22, of Centerdale, Rhode Island; Staff Sergeant Francis K. Sutek, 35, of Fort Walton Beach, Florida; and Technical Sergeant Eddie Miller, 36, of Rienzi, Mississippi.

Boxing was used for training as well as recreation and served to release some steam while also giving those who wished to gamble something to wager on.

The peace movement was not confined to college campuses back in the U.S. Many soldiers, especially among those drafted, grew increasingly disillusioned with the war and longed for it to end.

A crewman of an M113 relaxes near An Loc on Christmas Day, 1968.

A soldier of the 23rd Infantry Division (Americal) relaxes with his guitar while on R&R, May 1969. The Americal's reputation was severely tarnished by the actions of a single platoon which, led by Lt. William Calley, killed Vietnamese civilians at the village of My Lai in March 1968.

Obscured by darkness (and perhaps thankfully so), human waste from latrines is burnt with gasoline at LZ Sally in May 1968. Without adequate plumbing and sewage removal, burning waste was crucial in order to keep diseases such as cholera at bay.

Soldiers play cards while waiting. The war, while often frantic, could also be boring. The refusal of the enemy to engage in set-piece battles meant that much time was spent traveling the breadth and width of South Vietnam looking for them—and often sitting and waiting for the enemy to come to them.

Though blurry, the sentiment comes through loud and clear. Going home was the most important day of a soldier's tour. August 1969.

A Sky Trooper from the 1st Cavalry Division (Airmobile) keeps track of the time he has left on his "short time" helmet while participating in Operation Pershing, near Bong Son, 1968. Unlike previous wars, in which entire units shipped out together and remained a cohesive unit until the conflict was won, the draft system employed during the Vietnam War created a complex affair that created individual tours of duty. U.S. ARMY

It was a glorious day when a soldier could hop a bird back to the World. In the spring of 1966, Pan Am began flying American troops from Vietnam to R&R destinations all over South East Asia as well as to Japan and, later, Hawaii and Australia. In two years it flew more than 500,000 passengers on R&R flights alone. June 1968.

Newly freed prisoners of war celebrate as their C-141A aircraft lifts off from Hanoi, North Vietnam, on February 12, 1973, during Operation Homecoming. The mission included fifty-four C-141 flights between February 12 and April 4, 1973, returning 591 POWs to American soil. U.S. AIR FORCE

APPENDIX:
U.S. ARMY AND TOTAL U.S.
MILITARY PERSONNEL
IN SOUTH VIETNAM

Date	U.S. Army Personnel	Total U.S. Military Personnel
31 Dec 1960	800	900
31 Dec 1961	2,100	3,200
31 Dec 1962	7,900	11,300
31 Dec 1963	10,100	16,300
31 Dec 1964	14,700	23,300
31 Mar 1965	15,600	29,100
30 Jun	27,300	59,900
30 Sep	76,200	132,300
31 Dec	116,800	184,300
31 Mar 1966	137,400	231,200
30 Jun	160,000	267,500
30 Sep	189,200	313,100
31 Dec	239,400	485,300
31 Mar 1967	264,600	420,900
30 Jun	285,700	448,800
30 Sep	296,100	459,700
31 Dec	319,500	485,600
31 Mar 1968	337,300	515,200
30 Jun	354,300	534,700
30 Sep	354,200	537,800
31 Dec	359,800	536,100
31 Jan 1969*	365,600	542,400
31 Mar	361,500	538,200
30 Jun	360,500	538,700
30 Sep	345,400	510,500
31 Dec	330,300	474,400
31 Mar 1970	321,400	448,500
30 Jun	297,800	413,900
30 Sep	295,400	394,100
31 Dec	250,700	335,800
31 Mar 1971	227,600	301,900
3 Jun	197,500	250,900

From *Vietnam Studies Logistics Support* by Lieutenant General Joseph M. Heiser Jr.

---

*Indicates peak strength in South Vietnam.

ACKNOWLEDGMENTS

The following people deserve credit for their generous assistance. In each and every case, they went above and beyond to help bring this book to life by offering their expertise and time: Ted G. Arthurs, Robert W. Black, John Brennan, Larry Chambers, Jim Haley, Reginald Hathorn, Michael Lee Lanning, Gary Linderer, Mike McCarthy, Jim Ross, and Dave Walker; and, at Stackpole, Dave Reisch, Wendy Reynolds, and Brittany Stoner.

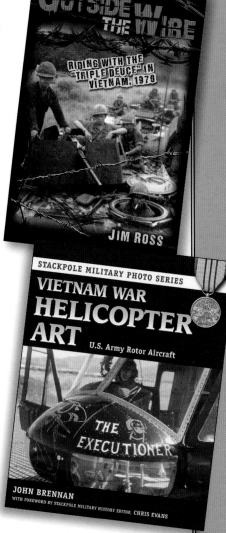

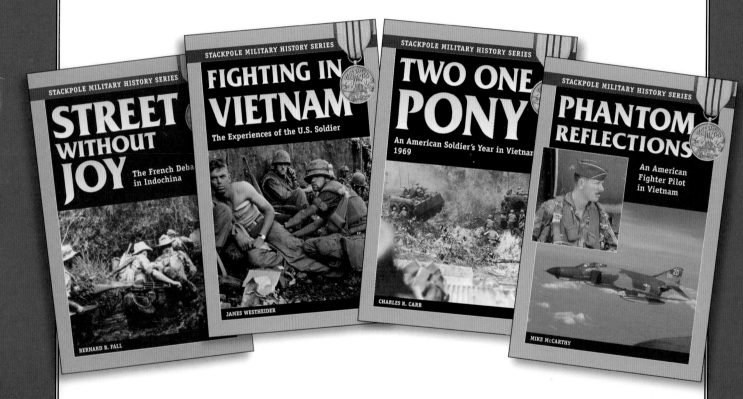